Introduc

T he **Black Mountains** are the first and la: top of the easternmost ridge, and astric a line was drawn here. To the east lie the fe. midlands. To the west, a succession of untame horizon. On the northern edge is a spectacular ... across the Wye Valley to Mid Wales. A series of tops ..... this ridge, and form the most impressive profile of the range. However these tops turn out to be just the terminal elevations of five main ridges stretching up to fifteen miles south, like fingers reaching out from knuckles.

The Black Mountains are made chiefly of Old Red Sandstone. At lower levels there is an abundance of vegetation. Natural woodland includes alder, beech, hazel, oak and birch. Wild flowers grow in profusion in hedgerows that are centuries old. The slopes of the mountains are convex, rising steeply out of the valleys but gradually easing up to the long ridges covered in heather, bilberry or bracken. Therefore on most walks the steepest climbing comes first. The reward is often a long, gentle and uninterrupted ridge walk with spectacular views. *However, mountain precautions should always be taken on these remote and unsheltered heights.*

There are a few small settlements but no real villages within the mountains. Abergavenny is the key town in the area, offering a wide range of facilities and good bus and rail connections. Other centres include Crickhowell, Hay and Talgarth.

The Black Mountains abound with historical interest and mystery. Myths and legends imbue the walks with a sense of mystery from the dawn of time. The area was probably settled during the Stone Age around 2500BC. Some standing stones date from the era of the Beaker folk, who migrated to the area from Europe after about 1700BC. Iron Age forts were built from about 250BC and confirm the strategic importance of hilltops. **Walk 5** visits Dinas Castell, **Walk 16** Crug Hywel near Crickhowell and **Walk 14** Twyn-y-Gaer. The Normans made their mark on the region, often using more ancient fortified sites. Longtown Castle (**Walk 8**) and Tretower are examples (**Walk 10**). The influence of Christianity underpins the history of these hills. St David himself established a church on the site of Llanthony Priory (**Walks 3, 4 & 7**), while the ancient well at Patrishow recalls a Celtic saint (**Walk 6**).

But perhaps the most exhilarating experience is walking the broad, open tops such as the border ridge (**Walks 7, 8 & 13**) or Mynydd Llangorse (**Walks 10 & 19**). This is unspoilt and spectacular country waiting to set you free.

Warning: Many of these walks cross open moorland, and on these 'mountain precautions' should always be taken. Ensure that you are appropriately dressed (*with extra clothing in your rucksack even in summer*), have good walking boots, a compass and basic emergency equipment. And don't forget to take some energy food and drink.

RHOS DIRION FROM RHOS FACH

DESCRIPTION A 5½-mile circular walk around the Black Mountains' dramatic northern escarpment. An ancient road across the range offers a clear line of ascent. The effort is rewarded with outstanding views along an easy traverse of the ridge. The return route follows a lovely descent through bracken and gorse along the base of the mountains' steep buttresses.
START Rhos Fach Common. SO 187334.
DIRECTIONS Rhos Fach Common lies about two miles east of Talgarth along a minor road. The road starts in the centre of the town, opposite the Coop, and passes an old hospital before gaining a shelf of land below the Black Mountains escarpment. Rhos Fach Common is open land and it is easy to leave a car on firm grass at the side of the road. *This walk includes high level moorland. You should take appropriate equipment, including navigation aids.*

I FOLLOW A WIDE GRASSY TRACK eastwards heading towards the hillside. *This is actually an old road traversing the Black Mountains via the Grwyne Fawr valley on the other side of the escarpment. Hence the sign at the beginning banning all vehicles except 'motorcycles with or without sidecars'. You may well feel that a ride in a sidecar over this terrain would be an experience worth missing! The environment is largely one of rough grassland but there are signs of ancient agriculture and the remains of some strip fields in the area.* Follow the track and cross a stile next to a conifer plantation. Continue on the track as it veers left through bracken and gorse to follow the line of a wire fence up the hillside. The fence remains our companion until we gain the summit plateau, though it is not marked on OS maps. The track becomes more eroded and less grassy but is a steady ascent, offering widening views over Talgarth and beyond to the Wye Valley. After a while it curves right to

climb up the side of the deep, rocky defile of Cwm Cwnstab. After a double bend in the track, the gradient eases before a final ascent to the top of the escarpment.

2 As you reach the head of the cwm, the path veers left following the line of the fence. About 100 yards further, GO LEFT through a gate in the fence leaving the old track which continues across the moor towards Grwyne Fawr reservoir. *The new path ascends gently across grassy terrain, which is intermittently soggy. There are views south down the Grwyne Fawr valley and on to Pen y Gadair Fawr and Waun Fach. Soon views open out northwards over the Wye Valley.*

3 The summit of the walk is reached at a trig point on Rhos Dirion, marking a height of 713m. *This is also the highest point on the Black Mountains' impressive northern escarpment, though apart from this topographical detail the summit itself is little more than a featureless grassy swelling on the edge of the moor. The same certainly cannot be said of the view from here, which includes a wide swathe of Mid Wales extending from Carmarthen Fan and the Brecon Beacons in the west to Radnor Forest in the north.* From here, the route continues along the edge of the escarpment, now following a gentle but steady descent until the path reaches the head of a deep defile at Rhiw y Fan. Follow the path carefully around this as it curves slightly to the left. About 400 yards further on reach a junction. It is clear on the ground, but would be easy to miss if concentration lapses, so watch out. (If you want to extend the walk slightly and climb to the top of Twmpa, continue forward. The summit lies about 700 yards ahead up a gentle climb. Retrace your steps to this point to rejoin the circuit.)

4 At the junction, take the track that SLANTS LEFTWARDS descending below the escarpment. This is a bridleway that has crossed the mountains from the Vale of Ewyas and now drops gently down the northern slopes of the range. After another 400 yards, the track turns back sharply to

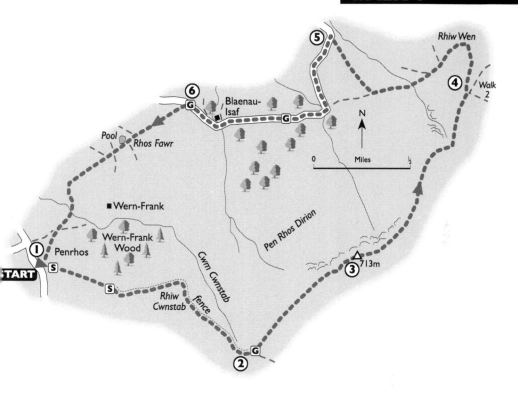

the left and becomes a grassy passageway through ferns. Ahead in the distance lie the peaks of the Brecon Beacons. *To the left you can now see the escarpment from below, with the impressive exposed red sandstone strata giving the Black Mountains their distinctive profile.* Continue to follow the line of this path, ignoring turn offs to the right (the line of the bridleway is one of these turn-offs). A little further on, just above a reedy gully, the path curves to the right and descends gently to join a tarmac lane just by a ford.

5 TURN LEFT here and follow the lane as it weaves through bracken and then turns sharp right over a stream. It continues through a grove of alder trees to reach a gate. Pass through the gate and continue along the road, descending to the farmhouse at Blaenau-isaf. The road climbs from the house

and soon reaches a gate giving access to open land.

6 Go through the gate, then BEAR LEFT, leaving the road to follow a path across the common land, Rhos Fawr. Maintain this direction across the heath, with Pen y Fan, the highest peak of the Beacons, directly ahead in the distance. Pass a small pond and soon pick up the line of a fence, following this on its right hand side. The path drops into a small valley and picks up a track. Follow this left, soon leading through a gate and crossing a stream. The track becomes a sunken lane, which can be muddy but this shortly emerges back on to open heath land. This is now Rhos Fach. Continue across a stony track, keeping to the grassy path in line with the fence. This brings you back to the starting point.

3

TWMPA, NANT BWCH & DARREN LWYD

DESCRIPTION This 6 mile walk starts in the idyllic hamlet of Capel-y-ffin, nestling in the upper reaches of the Honddu valley. An initial steep climb up the ridge of Darren Lwyd is rewarded with splendid views and much gentler walking to the summit of Twmpa on the northern escarpment of the Black Mountains. The return route follows the charming valley of Nant Bwch until it joins the Honddu back at Capel-y-ffin. *A high level walk requiring appropriate precautions.*

START Capel-y-ffin. SO 255314. An alternative start is at Gospel Pass GR SO 236351.

DIRECTIONS The village is situated on the minor road between Hay and Abergavenny. This joins the A465 at Llanfihangel Crucorney. It is a scenic but narrow route crossing the Gospel Pass at 538 metres above sea level. Note that parking is very limited in Capel-y-ffin. There are a few spaces on the verges or where the lane widens, but these can be taken quickly at weekends. The alternative start at Gospel Pass offers easier parking. There is a car park at the side of the road here, just south of its highest point. A clear track leads from the summit of the road, following the escarpment to the summit of Twmpa. Then follow the instructions from Point **2.** This adds just over a mile to the total distance.

*C*apel-y-ffin *lies near the head of the Honddu valley, at the river's confluence with Nant Bwch. Its name means 'Chapel of the Boundary', situated in the far north of Monmouthshire, close to its border with Brecknock, now Powys. Its peaceful setting, deep in a fertile, wooded valley has attracted many people. A Roman Catholic priest, Father Ignatius, founded a monastery here in 1869. In 1924 the buildings were taken over by Eric Gill who established a self-sufficient religious community. He worked as a sculptor and calligrapher, devising 11 new fonts, the best known of which is Gill Sans (one of the typefaces in this book). 'The Monastery' can still be seen on the side of the hill to the west of the village, though there is no public access.*

From the bridge follow the road northwards towards Hay, passing the white painted church on your right. *This is St Mary's, part of the Church in Wales. It was built in 1762 and includes an eighteenth century pulpit and a medieval font. It is one of the smallest churches in Wales, measuring 25 feet by 12 feet.* In about 300 yards, by a sign to the Grange Trekking Centre, a public footpath sign indicates a route LEFT over a stile and then through a gate. This path ascends a field towards a house. The steep ridge of Darren Lwyd looms up before you. At the top of the field cross a stile and then pass between the house and a converted barn. The right of way goes straight on, through a clear gap in the hedge, and then to a gate leading to open country. A steep stony path begins the assault of Darren Lwyd, following the line of a fence. Where the fence veers to the left, by an ash tree, TURN SHARP RIGHT and follow a narrow path ascending through bracken. Keep to this narrow but clear path as it maintains this line, climbing diagonally across the side of the hill, ignoring any tracks that cross it. After a while, above the buildings of Trwyn-tal below you, the path swings sharply left and continues its diagonal ascent in the opposite direction. Soon you gain the nape of the ridge and the path turns right to climb directly up to a cairn on the skyline. *It's not quite the top, but the worst is over, and you can afford to pause and enjoy the views back over Capel-y-ffin and the Vale of Ewyas. Notice the clear U-shape of the valley, carved not by the River Honddu alone, but also by glacial erosion.* A much gentler ascent now lies ahead as the path crowns the ridge of Darren Lwyd. The valley road can be seen snaking up towards the Gospel Pass and, on the left, there are views across Nant Bwch to the highest land of the Black Mountains. The path keeps more or less to the crest of the ridge and, where this broadens, maintain your course across the moor to gain the summit of Twmpa, where the ground abruptly falls away to the Wye Valley. *Twmpa's alias,*

Twmpa
(Lord Hereford's Knob)

△ ②

③ Walk 1

ALTERNATIVE START Ⓟ

N ↑

Darren Lwyd

Afon Honddu

0 — Miles — ½

Capel-y-ffin hostel

Trwyn-tal

Talsarn ■

Pen-y-maes Ⓖ Ⓢ

The Grange

The Monastery ①

Walk 4

Ⓖ Ⓢ **Capel-y-ffin**

Walk 4

START

place to picnic. A gate leads from the open country on to a surfaced lane, passing the farmhouse of Blaen-bwch. It soon descends through woods. This is a very quiet lane and a pleasure to walk. Hedges provide a fertile habitat for wild flowers such as the abundant Herb Robert. The lane leads gently down to Capel-y-ffin passing a riding centre as you enter the hamlet.

Lord Hereford's Knob, attracts speculation and innuendo. But the allusion appears to be only to a topographical description of a local neighbourhood owned by a local aristocrat! In 1998 the band Half Man Half Biscuit made the peak's name into a title of a song. Even the grid reference found its way into the lyrics. Enjoy the truly panoramic views, this time northwards across the Wye Valley to Radnor Forest and beyond. (If you started the walk at Gospel Pass, turn right and retrace your steps down to the road).

2 At the summit cairn, TURN LEFT and follow the path down from the summit. Where paths diverge, keep to the route nearest to the edge of the escarpment, as this will aid navigation.

3 A stony track leads sharply down to the right to drop down diagonally from the ridge. In the opposite direction a grassy path crosses the moor. TURN LEFT to follow this. It soon descends gently towards the valley of Nant Bwch, crossing the infant stream and keeping to the left hand bank. *The stream drops more steeply than the path, so soon you have a pleasant view down the increasingly vertiginous banks clothed with ferns, bilberries and heather. The path is reunited with the stream near a waterfall, an idyllic*

There are actually two chapels at Capel-y-ffin. The whitewashed building of the Church in Wales stands next to the road by the bridge. Its tiny gallery offers an aerial view of the church and the pulpit dates from 1786. The Baptist chapel lies a short way along the lane behind and was built in 1737. Above Capel-y-ffin, the road narrows and begins to climb the upper reaches of the Honddu valley to the Gospel Pass, an alternative start to Walk 2. The pass stands at 1778 feet above sea level, making this road the second highest in Wales.

THE VALE OF EYWAS

DESCRIPTION Llanthony Priory lies in a wild and beautiful setting, cocooned among the trees and hedgerows of the Vale of Ewyas, immediately below the steep, bracken clad ridge rising up to the English border less than a mile away. The remote hamlet of Capel-y-ffin is 4 miles further up the valley. **Walks 3** and **4** link the two hamlets of Llanthony and Capel-y-ffin by varying routes. This makes it possible to combine different legs of each walk to suit your taste or energy. This walk (8½ miles) starts with a climb up the attractive valley of Cwm Bwchel and leads to a cairn at Bal-Bach, marking the summit of a mountain pass. An old bridleway contours the side of the ridge, offering views across Llanthony and its historic ruins, before descending to Capel-y-ffin. The return journey travels along the bottom of the valley, making use of paths and little used lanes. The woods and hedgerows create their own natural haven for wild life and plants.

START Llanthony Priory. SO 289278.

DIRECTIONS Llanthony lies on a minor road between Llanfihangel Crucorney, on the A465 Abergavenny-Hereford road, and Hay-on-Wye. There is a car park at Llanthony Priory. There are also toilets here, and a pub.

*C*hristian worship *first took place at Llanthony over 1400 years ago when St David himself founded a chapel. The present remains date from the Norman period, when William de Lacy established a priory in about 1118. Later that century, Gerald of Wales visited Llanthony as part of his tour of Wales, recruiting soldiers for the Crusades. He commented it was situated among 'barbarous people'. The priory never really flourished. By the time of the dissolution of the monasteries in 1536, there were just four monks and the site was sold for less than £200. It is one of the best medieval buildings in Wales. It certainly occupies a classic position, and was painted by Turner on a visit in the nineteenth century.*

I Follow the priory access road back to the lane along the valley. To your left, on the opposite side of the lane, is a footpath sign to Bal-Bach. FOLLOW THE FOOTPATH, which goes to the right of the phone box, just in front of Mill House. Cross the River Honddu on a footbridge. On the far side of the bridge, turn right and cross a stile heading for Bal-Bach. Soon another stile leads into a muddy green lane. Thankfully cross over this, passing through a gate on the opposite side, to follow the signpost for Cwm Bwchel. Marker posts now lead you up through fields, crossing stiles and a small stream. The route then follows the right hand side of the stream up past the farm buildings at Cwm Bwchel to gain the open mountainside by a stile. Climb steadily up the side of the little valley with thorn trees and bracken giving colour and interest and the sound of the stream accompanying you all the way. Views of the priory and its surroundings offer a photogenic rear view as height is gained. As it emerges from the cwm, the path continues to climb through wilder, open country. It is now less steep and an engineered route spares you the bracken and squelchy peat.

2 At the cairn at Bal-Bach, TURN RIGHT to follow a broad track. After about 150 yards leave this track. (*It is the line of Walk 4 up to Bal-Mawr.*) Instead FORK RIGHT along a grassy track that contours around the side of the hill. The path is level at first and then descends gently. As it rounds the valley of Nant-y-Carnau, it drops more steeply. Eventually you come to a gate and pass through this into some trees.

3 Continue through a small wooded area. Beyond this the path contours the side of the hill with bracken covering the unenclosed slopes above. Eventually, just after crossing a small stream, your path joins the track descending from Blacksmith's Anvil and Chwarel-y-Fan (see Walk 4). The stony and eroded track now leads down to emerge onto a lane by a trekking centre. TURN RIGHT to reach Capel-y-ffin. (*See Walk 2 for more details about this remote hamlet.*)

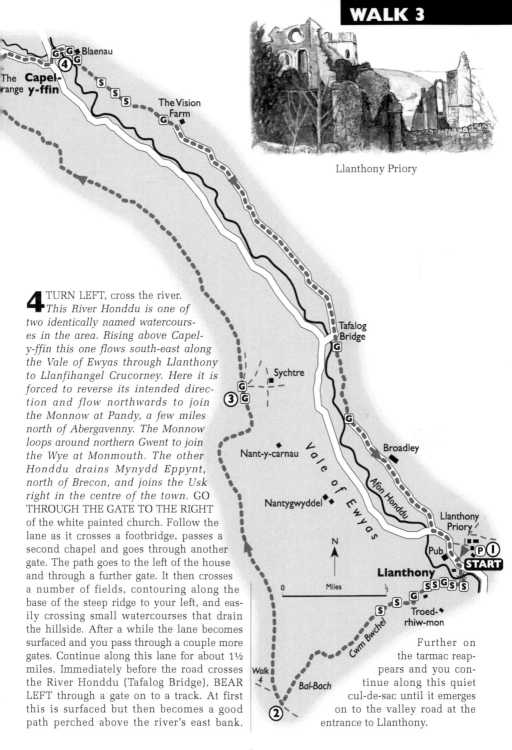

Llanthony Priory

Blaenau

The Capel-
range y-ffin

The Vision
Farm

Tafalog
Bridge

Sychtre

Nant-y-carnau

Vale of Ewyas

Broadley

Afôn Honddu

Nantygwyddel

Llanthony
Priory

N

Pub

START

Llanthony

0   Miles   ½

Troed-
rhiw-mon

Walk
4

Cwm Bwchel

Bal-Bach

4 TURN LEFT, cross the river. *This River Honddu is one of two identically named watercourses in the area. Rising above Capel-y-ffin this one flows south-east along the Vale of Ewyas through Llanthony to Llanfihangel Crucorney. Here it is forced to reverse its intended direction and flow northwards to join the Monnow at Pandy, a few miles north of Abergavenny. The Monnow loops around northern Gwent to join the Wye at Monmouth. The other Honddu drains Mynydd Eppynt, north of Brecon, and joins the Usk right in the centre of the town.* GO THROUGH THE GATE TO THE RIGHT of the white painted church. Follow the lane as it crosses a footbridge, passes a second chapel and goes through another gate. The path goes to the left of the house and through a further gate. It then crosses a number of fields, contouring along the base of the steep ridge to your left, and easily crossing small watercourses that drain the hillside. After a while the lane becomes surfaced and you pass through a couple more gates. Continue along this lane for about 1½ miles. Immediately before the road crosses the River Honddu (Tafalog Bridge), BEAR LEFT through a gate on to a track. At first this is surfaced but then becomes a good path perched above the river's east bank.

Further on the tarmac reappears and you continue along this quiet cul-de-sac until it emerges on to the valley road at the entrance to Llanthony.

WALK 4

CHWAREL-Y-FAN & OFFA'S DYKE PATH

DESCRIPTION A 9-mile walk exploring the upper reaches of the Vale of Eywas. Starting at the historic ruins of Llanthony Priory, the route ascends the delightful side valley of Cwm Bwchel to gain the Ffawyddog ridge. The ridge provides an airy and almost level traverse above the valley with extensive views across the whole of the Black Mountains. After the highest point, Chwarel-y-Fan, there is a descent to the isolated hamlet of Capel-y-ffin. The return leg entails a steep climb up the opposite ridge, followed by a stride along the border following Offa's Dyke Path (though not the dyke itself). The final descent offers classic views of the photogenic priory ruins. *This walk includes high moorland. You should take appropriate equipment including navigation aids.* Walks 3 and 4 link the two hamlets of Llanthony and Capel-y-ffin by varying routes. This makes it possible to combine different legs of each walk to suit your taste or energy.
START Llanthony Priory. SO 289278.
DIRECTIONS See **Walk 3**.

I The first part of the route follows **Walk 3** as far as Bal-Bach (instruction 1). *For historical background to Llanthony see Walk 3.*

2 A cairn marks the summit of the path. TURN RIGHT here to follow a broad track up the summit of Bal-Mawr, which is marked by a trig point. Continue beyond the summit on a clear path along the airy Ffawyddog ridge. *Enjoy views right over the Vale of Ewyas with Llanthony now far below. The Hatterall ridge on the far side of the valley marks the border with England, and also the line of Offa's Dyke long distance footpath. Leftwards, your eye is drawn across the afforested valley of the Grwyne Fawr to Pen y Gadair Fawr and Waun Fach, the highest of the Black Mountain summits beyond (see Walk 17).* The ridge provides a steady and easy walk, with slight undulations at Bwlch Isaf and Bwlch Bach before making a slight ascent to the top of Chwarel-y-Fan, marked by a large cairn at over 670 metres. Gently descend from the summit. In just over ½ mile reach a cairn marking a fork in the path.

3 This junction is known as the Blacksmith's Anvil. TAKE THE RIGHT FORK. The path descends gently at first, and then becomes more steep and rocky as it passes over the side of the ridge. Capel-y-ffin can now be seen below, with the ruins of the monastery clearly visible. Reach a grassy shelf, cross a stream and descend to the left of a conifer wood on an increasingly eroded track. The route emerges on to a lane by a trekking centre. TURN RIGHT, soon reaching the road junction and bridge at Capel-y-ffin. *See* **Walk 2** *for more information about this hamlet.*

4 Cross the river and GO THROUGH THE GATE TO THE RIGHT of the white painted church. Follow the lane as it crosses a footbridge, passes a second chapel and goes through another gate. The path goes to the left of the house and through a further gate. It then crosses a number of fields, contouring along the base of the steep ridge to your left, and easily crossing small watercourses that drain the hillside. After a while the lane becomes surfaced and you pass through a couple more gates. Immediately after the second gate, you leave the lane and turn SHARP LEFT over a stile at a signpost to 'The Hill' and 'Offa's Dyke'. Yellow waymarks indicate the route RIGHT towards the farm and then steeply LEFT straight up the hillside. A stile leads into some beech and ash woodland and the path continues relentlessly up hill. At the top of the wood, a stile leads to open countryside and the path turns RIGHT for a brief level section. Shortly, the path turns back to the LEFT renewing its resolve to conquer the ridge and reach the border on the top. The path is steep as it snakes its way through the bracken, which can be quite high in late summer, but the way is clear enough. Eventually the convex slope eases and the ferns give way to grass, clues that your labour is nearly complete.

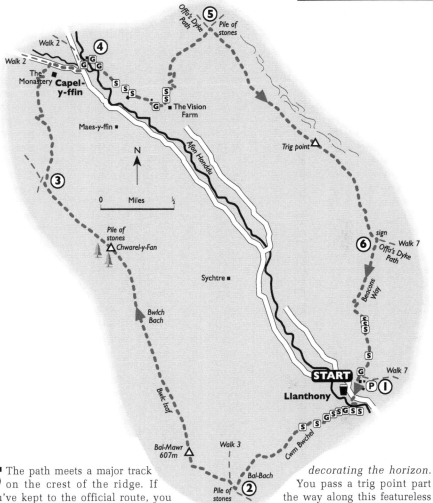

5 The path meets a major track on the crest of the ridge. If you've kept to the official route, you should join it at a pile of stones, but, even if you've strayed a bit, you will not miss the track. TURN RIGHT and follow it south, enjoying an extensive panorama over a wide area. *This is Offa's Dyke Long Distance Footpath on its way from Chepstow to Prestatyn. This ridge makes a splendid course for the footpath. It is easy to see why the border runs here, perhaps more than anywhere else along its length. To the west lie tiers of mountains parading into the interior of Wales, wild, rugged and confusing to an invader. To the east, the fertile fields of Herefordshire lead to the English Midlands, the outlines of the Malverns and Cotswolds* *decorating the horizon.* *You pass a trig point part the way along this featureless ridge.*

6 A sign to Llanthony on a stone slab marks the point where the path to the valley leaves the ridge. TURN RIGHT here. The descent is gentle at first but soon becomes much steeper as the ruins of the priory come into view over the brow of the hill. Although the gradient is serious, the path is clear and easy to negotiate and eventually a stile leads off the open access land. Descend the field beyond it and then cross two more stiles with a small copse between them. More fields lead gently down towards the historic walls of the priory and the starting point.

Y GRIB
& WAUN FACH

DESCRIPTION The highest castle in Wales and England and the highest point in the Black Mountains are both visited on this 7-mile expedition. A short but steep climb leads to Dinas Castell, which commands the top of the Rhiangoll valley, a strategic pass through the mountains between Mid and South Wales. From here an appealing walk up the switchback ridge of Y Grib leads to the summit plateau. This commands stunning views from the Cotswolds to Carmarthenshire, and swells gently to the top of Waun Fach. The return route descends the ridge of Pen Trumau and turns down an old route traversing the fell side into the valley below. *The walk includes remote moorland and mountain terrain, which require proper clothing and equipment as well as competent use of navigation aids in misty weather. **Take a compass.***

START Castle Inn, Pengenffordd SO 174297.

DIRECTIONS The Castle Inn is situated just south of the highest point on the A479 between Abergavenny and Talgarth. There is a large pub car park on the southbound side of the road, immediately north of the Castle Inn. Non-patrons are asked to pay a small charge for parking.

I From the northern end of the car park, follow the sign to Castell Dinas leading down some steps to a bridleway. TURN RIGHT along this lane for 50 yards and then cross a stile on the LEFT. Follow the side of the field to another stile, crossing this and a small stream. A steep ascent then faces you up to the top of Castell Dinas. Climb two fields, keeping the fence on your left. A third field, this time with the fence on your right brings you to the castle site.

2 Reaching the summit ridge, you TURN LEFT and the path weaves its way through the remains of the castle, which consists mainly of some mounds. *The original fort dates from the Iron Age and there was probably a Welsh stronghold here. The site*
commands the top of the Rhiangoll valley, a key pass between the Usk and Wye valleys. The Normans made use of the position in the twelfth century. Some of their ditches and ramparts still evident today, although little remains of any masonry.* At the end of the castle site, the path descends, crossing a defensive ditch and passing an old well, until it reaches the saddle. Cross the stile, which gives access to the open mountainside. The beginning of the Dragon's Back ridge (or Y Grib) now lies directly before you. Avoid the tracks either side of the ridge and take the grassy path more or less up the centre as it weaves its way through bracken. A small wind shelter marks the top of the first part of the 'Dragon's Back'. Descend a little way to the next col and continue like this on up the ridge, keeping where possible to the crest for greatest effect, though alternative routes sometimes lurch slightly to the side. *Gliders may accompany you from the nearby flying club as they swoop up above the highest land and use the thermal currents to return to the airfield.*

3 At the top of a rock section a significant cairn marks the top of Y Grib and the beginning of more open mountain country. Care is now needed to find the right route. In clear weather there will be no problem. You are simple aiming for the slight elevation on the ridge in front of you, which is Pen y Manllwyn and it doesn't really matter which course you follow to get there. However, in misty weather navigation will be important. About 50 yards after the cairn, there is a faint bifurcation in the path, which is easy to miss. The more prominent left hand fork leads around the edge of the steepest slopes to Y Das. However, our route takes the RIGHT HAND FORK on a bearing of 90 degrees. A small pile of stones about 10 yards after the junction confirms your choice and the path heads across the shoulder of land, with some wet patches in places. Once on the path, it's clear enough to follow and after a while it ascends more steeply. The path emerges on to the ridge track just north of Pen y Manllwyn, though short cuts may lead you straight to its 'summit', a slight soggy swelling.

4 TURN RIGHT and and follow the wide and boggy 'path' along the broad ridge, negotiating peaty channels from time to time. The route is generally level until the short final ascent to the summit of Waun Fach. *This is the highest point in the Black Mountains at 810 metres, but*

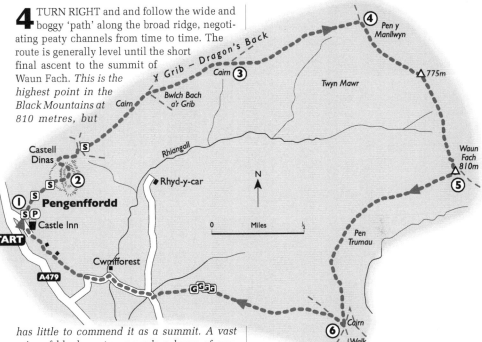

has little to commend it as a summit. A vast mire of black peat surrounds a lump of concrete. Even the OS has turned its back on Waun Fach, preferring to grace other landmarks for triangulation surveys. However, the views are more than adequate compensation for Waun Fach's other inadequacies. Eastwards the panorama stretches across the rest of the Black Mountains to the Clee Hills in Shropshire and the Cotswolds in Gloucestershire; southwards across the Bristol Channel to distant Exmoor; westwards far across Wales to Carmarthen Fan and beyond.

5 At the summit, TURN RIGHT and follow a course west-south-west (240 degrees). You will need a compass in poor visibility, as the path is not evident from the peaty quagmire of the summit. However, it becomes clear after a few yards and from then on you should have no route finding problems. A steady but easy descent leads along the ridge to Pen Trumau, with views back to Y Grib and Dinas Castell to your right. Follow the broad crest of the ridge as it turns in a more southerly direction. A steeper and rockier section leads to a narrow saddle of land at the col between Waun Fach and Mynydd Llysiau

6 A cairn marks the junction of paths at this idyllic mountain pass. Walk 15 links here. Our route requires you to TURN SHARP RIGHT. The track slants down across the hillside and in about 200 yards be careful to follow the main path as it BEARS LEFT to descend directly down the mountain. (Avoid the contouring path ahead). The gradient steepens and the path becomes stonier as the Rhiangoll valley comes fully into view below. *Thorn trees and bracken now accompany you on a charming terrace path.* A series of gates herald entry into enclosed land and a fenced lane leads down to a tarmac side road. TURN RIGHT and in 50 yards BEAR LEFT. The lane drops down to cross the Rhiangoll and passes a riding centre. 300 yards after the riding centre, the lane bends sharply back to the left. At this point, carry STRAIGHT AHEAD on to a rather muddy track. Cross a small ford and carry on up the bridleway as it ascends gently, parallel to the main road. It soon leads back to the steps, which return you to the car park and the start of the walk.

WALK 6

THE VALLEY OF THE GRWYNE FAWR

DESCRIPTION The story of a saint and a murderer endow this walk with mystery and heritage from the mists of time. The 5-mile circuit of the middle reaches of the Grwyne Fawr valley starts along good tracks through Mynydd Du forest. Once in open country a traverse of the lower slopes of Crug Mawr offers a panorama across the valley. Pause at Patrishow, an ancient church perched on an isolated hillside and dedicated to St Issui. Pilgrims still visit the well of this early Celtic saint, hidden in trees just below the church. The return route crosses the river and follows its eastern side, with good views back across the Grwyne Fawr.

START Car park at Pont Cadwgan accessed by a bridge across the river from the valley road. SO 267252.

DIRECTIONS The valley road is a cul-de-sac, which starts at the crossroads at Forest Coalpit. It follows the Grwyne Fawr river northwards deep into the heart of the Black Mountains. Forest Coalpit can be accessed by narrow lanes from Crickhowell or by leaving the A465 at Llanfihangel Crucorney, four miles north of Abergavenny.

I Go back to the car park entrance and cross the road. Follow a forestry road slanting uphill through the trees. After about half a mile come to a junction of forest roads and BEAR LEFT, following a sign to Ffordd-las-fawr. Continue on this level track through the woods. *Enjoy the variety of trees here, with a range of deciduous species surviving the onward march of the ubiquitous conifer.* Continue STRAIGHT ON at another junction of bridleways and continue with the track as it curves over a stream and passes between derelict buildings at Ffordd-las fawr. *This valley used to be much more populous than today. Until the nineteenth century over 30 farmsteads provided a livelihood for its inhabitants.* At the far end of the buildings

TURN LEFT. In 150 yards keep straight on at a junction of bridleways, continuing on the level path, now narrower.

2 Soon a gate marks the end of the forest and leads immediately to a mountain stream. Fording this may be difficult if it is in full spate after heavy rain. However, there is an easier step across a few yards upstream. On the other side of the stream FOLLOW THE BRIDLEWAY LEFT up the side of the hill. It follows the wall marking the boundary of open land and gradually curves round to become parallel to the Grwyne Fawr valley. At the end of the open countryside, pass two gates and a sheepfold on to a green lane between two fences. This soon leads to a tarmac lane. TURN RIGHT and descend steeply to the tiny church at Patrishow. You can enter the churchyard by a stile or the lych gate. *There is evidence that a church may have been established here before the time of William the Conqueror and the inscription on the font has been dated to about 1055. According to legend, it was financed by an outsider as an offering of thanks for a cure from leprosy. The nave may be Norman and the screen and rood loft date from around 1400.* The road continues down to a bridge. *Just beside this is St Issui's Well (Ffynnon Ishow). This early Christian priest lived near the well and offered hospitality to travellers. He was murdered by one such itinerant and his well has since been a site of Celtic pilgrimage for centuries. The small spring, framed by stone, lies down a few steps amidst the trees, usually adorned with flowers or greenery.*

3 From the well, turn back towards the church but immediately TURN RIGHT over a stile. The path follows the bottom of the field below the church to reach another stile. This gives access to a lane. Pass to the right of a white farmhouse and continue down to the valley road. TURN LEFT and walk along the road carefully for about 300 yards. At a sign to Tabernacle Chapel BEAR RIGHT down the lane, which curves right to cross the river. You pass the Tabernacle Baptist chapel to your left. An inscription dates this to 1837. Follow the lane around

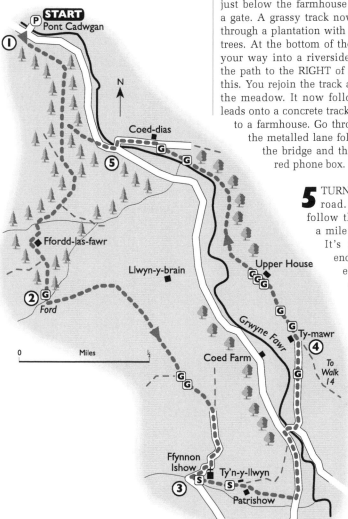

just below the farmhouse and pass through a gate. A grassy track now leads down hill through a plantation with a variety of young trees. At the bottom of the track a gate bars your way into a riverside meadow. Follow the path to the RIGHT of the fence to avoid this. You rejoin the track at the other end of the meadow. It now follows the river and leads onto a concrete track that then ascends to a farmhouse. Go through the gate onto the metalled lane following it down to the bridge and the valley road by a red phone box.

5 TURN RIGHT along the road. You can simply follow the road for about a mile back to the start. It's quiet and wide enough to avoid close encounters with any traffic there is. If you don't like road walking, BEAR LEFT in 100 yards to follow a footpath sign. You climb back into the woods to join the forest road that was our outward route. TURN RIGHT and descend back to the car park. *The road along the valley was only completed in 1912 as part of a reservoir construction project. The Grwyne Fawr Reservoir at the head of the valley was completed in 1928. It was built to provide water for the area around Abertillery in the Western Valley of Monmouthshire. A temporary town, Blaen-y-cwm, was built to house the workers. You can visit the reservoir by continuing along the valley road to its terminus where another car park is provided (see Walk 17).*

to the LEFT as it climbs the side of the valley. Just past the gate take the upper track signposted to Upper House, passing above Ty Mawr farmhouse.

4 *From Ty Mawr, the path leading up sharply to the right leads to Twyn-y-Gaer. It links with point 5 on* **Walk 14** *if you want to extend the walk to visit the ancient fort.* To continue with this walk, ignore the turning and ascend the lane ahead to Upper House. Here, ignore another right hand turn to 'The Hill', instead carry STRAIGHT ON

13

WALK 7

UP TO THE BORDER

DESCRIPTION This is a classic circular walk, 5 miles in length. It starts from the atmospheric ruins of Llanthony Abbey and climbs up the steep eastern side of the Honddu valley to gain the Hatterrall ridge and the English border. An easy walk leads north along the ridge, with extensive views across both sides of the border. The return leg descends from the ridge by a well-used path enjoying high-level views of the Priory ruins. This walk can be combined with **Walk 8** to make a fine 9-mile expedition over to the ancient settlement of Longtown on the English side of the ridge. To do this, track the instructions for this walk as far as point **3**. Then follow Walk 8 from point 3 into Longtown. Return by using Walk 8 from the start at Longtown to the border ridge, turning north to Point 4 on Walk 7 and the descent back to Llanthony.

START Llanthony Priory. SO 289278.

DIRECTIONS Llanthony Priory lies just over 6 miles off the A465 Between Abergavenny and Hereford. Turn off the main road ay Llanfihangel Crucorney and follow the valley road signposted to Llanthony. The starting point can also be reached from Hay on Wye via the minor road over the Gospel Pass. There are toilets and a car park at Llanthony Priory.

See Walk 3 for background details about Llanthony Priory.

I Leave the car park passing the abbey on your right and the church of St David on your left. Where the access road turns left down the hill, KEEP STRAIGHT AHEAD THROUGH A GATE AND TURN IMMEDIATELY RIGHT up the track signposted to Hatterrall Hill. At the end of the field go through another gate and immediately TURN RIGHT to follow a sign to 'Offa's Dyke South' above the perimeter of the abbey. At the end of the Abbey's wall go through another gate and BEAR LEFT to climb up the field diagonally. A gate at the top leads in to

a wood. Follow the track as it climbs through the trees. At the far end ignore the metal gate ahead. Instead GO THROUGH A WOODEN FIELD GATE TO THE LEFT and climb up the last field with the fence to your right. At the top a final gate leads on to the open hillside.

2 TURN RIGHT and follow the path signposted to Cwmyoy. At first you enjoy some respite as the path follows a level course along a shelf on the hillside, just above the boundary of enclosed land. It weaves through bracken and a scattering of trees before beginning to climb diagonally up the hillside. As you climb, enjoy views down the Vale of Ewyas and on to the Sugar Loaf. Near the upper reaches a wall joins you on the left and the gradient eases. Ignore a branch doubling back to the left and maintain the same direction slanting up the hill. You gain the crest of the ridge at a junction of paths marked with a stone direction post. *This ridge extends for 12 miles from Hatterrall Hill in the south to Hay Bluff, overlooking the Wye valley, in the north. It is the most easterly of the long ridges of the Black Mountains and marks the border between Wales and England for all of its length. It also carries Offa's Dyke Long Distance footpath. This 177-mile odyssey winds its way from Prestatyn to Chepstow, often following the line of the ninth century earthwork erected as a demarcation for Offa's Saxon kingdom. There is no evidence that the Dyke came along this ridge, though fragments have been found further east. However the ridge itself is a definitive border and makes an excellent high-level walk from Pandy to Hay-on-Wye. Ahead the path drops steeply down the others side into Longtown (see Walk 8). If you want to visit the summit of Hatterrall Hill, it's a short way to the right.*

3 *If you want to combine Walks 7 and 8 follow the instructions from point 3 on Walk 8 to descend to Longtown. But to follow Walk 7, TURN LEFT at the junction. An easy ascent leads to the trig point at 552m. There are extensive views here and all along the ridge. Down to the east lie the Monnow valley, Cloddock church and the straggling village of Longtown. Beyond are the rolling*

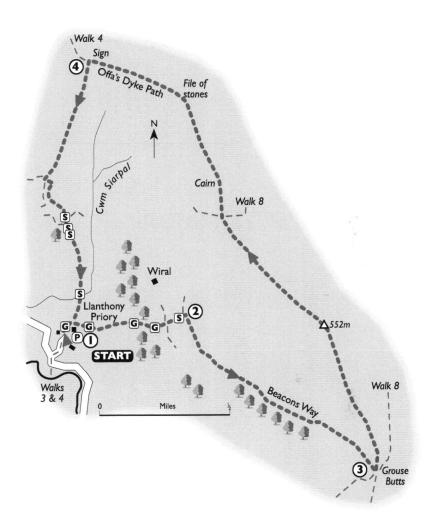

fields of Herefordshire with distant views to the Cotswolds and Clee Hills on a clear day. To the west, successive ridges of the Black Mountains march westwards into the hinterlands of Wales. This feels like a border. Continue beyond along the ridge for about 1¼ miles.

4 A stone direction post and a large cairn mark the turning point for Llanthony. On reaching this junction, TURN LEFT and follow the clear path. The descent is gentle at first but soon becomes much steeper as the ruins of the priory come into view over the brow of the hill. Although the gradient is serious, the path is clear and easy to negotiate and eventually a stile leads off the open access land. Descend the field beyond it and then cross two more stiles with a small copse between them. More fields lead gently down towards the historic walls of the priory and the starting point.

15

LONGTOWN & OFFA'S DYKE PATH

DESCRIPTION The old medieval settlement of Longtown lies sheltered beneath the looming heights of the Black Mountains. The village sits on a slight ridge between the River Monnow and the Olchon Brook on the Herefordshire side of the border. This 5-mile circuit of the border is the first of two walks that climb the eastern ridge of the Black Mountains from England. The first part of the ascent lies through fields rising from the Olchon Brook to the base of the Hatterrall ridge. A steep climb then takes you to the top of the ridge, which is the line of the border. An enjoyable walk follows the border south, also accompanying Offa's Dyke long distance path. Descent from the ridge uses an ancient cross-border track between Llanthony and Longtown. This walk can be combined with **Walk 7** to make a grand 9 mile excursion over the border ridge to Llanthony. To do this follow the walk to point 2 and on up to the ridge. Then see the note in the text below.

START Car park at Longtown Village Hall. SO 324287.

DIRECTIONS Longtown is reached by a minor road, which leaves the A465 at the Pandy Inn, about 6 miles north of Abergavenny. From the north leave the A465 at Pontrilas and travel by another minor road through Ewyas Harold.

Before or after your walk you may like to visit Longtown Castle, which lies a short way up the road from the Village Hall. It was built as an earthen enclosure in 1180 by Walter de Lacy. The impressive stone keep dates from the 13th century and was defended by walls over 4 yards thick. The town never really developed as intended and the castle was abandoned in the fourteenth century. It was briefly reoccupied during Owain Glyndwr's campaign for Welsh independence in the early 15th century. The castle is now cared for by English Heritage and there is free access at any reasonable time.

1 From the car park TURN LEFT to follow the road and soon TURN LEFT down a lane. Both 'speed limit ends' and 'no through road' signs mark its start, an interesting combination of rubrics. This lane soon descends to cross the Olchon Brook. Go through the gate on the far side. Soon after passing a static caravan, CROSS A STILE ON THE RIGHT into a field. Pass across the next three fields following a small stream on your right. At the top of the third field CROSS THE WOODEN FOOTBRIDGE and head across the next small field to a gap in the trees. Here BEAR LEFT to ascend the next field diagonally to a gate in the top corner. Don't go through this, instead stay inside the field and follow the fence. Keep ascending to pass through a gap in the next hedge, then reaching a track. FOLLOW THIS TO THE RIGHT, across a ford and on through some farm buildings to reach a road. TURN LEFT and follow the road as it winds up hill.

2 The road bends to the right just after a cattle grid. But at this point, leave the road and TURN LEFT along a green lane. In about 200 yards leave this to BEAR RIGHT up the hillside following a public footpath sign. Follow this well trodden path as it climbs diagonally leftwards above a small, enclosed copse. About 100 yards after you leave the company of this enclosure, the track crosses a sunken path. TURN RIGHT to follow this path as it slants diagonally up to the right. *The Hatterrall Ridge stretches northwards from Pandy past Longtown and towards Hay on Wye. Nowhere perhaps is the border between Wales and England more distinct than here. The fertile rolling hills of Herefordshire face the steep and daunting slopes of this ridge. Indeed some say that the formidable appearance of the hills from the east gave them the title of the Black Mountains.* About two-thirds the way up it doubles back to the left and continues its ascent. As it nears the top it veers right, becomes narrower and arrives at a wide path on the crest of the ridge by a small pile of stones. *To combine this walk with Walk 7 to Llanthony, turn right here and follow the ridge until you reach Point 4 on Walk 7 then following the instructions from Point 4 to*

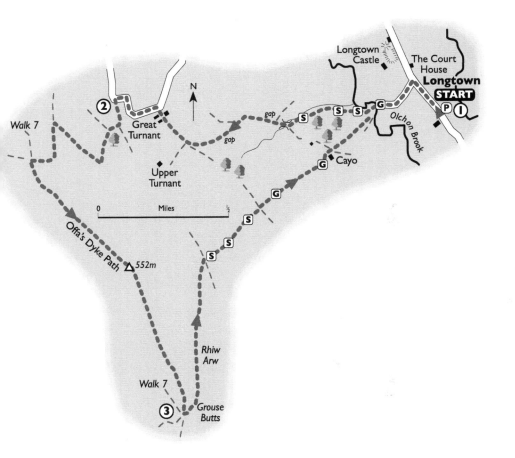

Llanthony. Otherwise TURN LEFT to follow the ridge south. It marks both the border and the line of the Offa's Dyke long distance path. Pass the trig point at a height of 552m. About ½-mile past this you descend slightly to a junction of paths. This is the ancient route between Llanthony Abbey and Longtown. The junction is marked by stone sign.

3 TURN LEFT to follow the path towards Longtown. The path immediately descends diagonally down the hill. Maintain this direction into you join a green lane which runs along the edge of the open coun-

try. Here the boundary fence dips down to a gateway. CROSS THE STILE next to it, giving access to a passage between two fences. At the bottom of this CROSS ANOTHER STILE and descend the next field to the bottom left corner. Carry on down the left hand side of the next few fields, adjacent to a line of trees and a fence. At the bottom of the last field a gate leads into a farmyard. Go through the farm buildings and on down the concrete access road to cross the Olchon brook. The lane now leads back into Longtown. At the road TURN RIGHT to return to your starting point or turn left to visit the castle first.

BLACK HILL

DESCRIPTION A genuine introduction to two common features of the Black Mountains: wild, bleak ridges and well-vegetated isolated valleys. The outward route climbs an airy serrated ridge known colloquially as the 'Cat's Back'. This splendid approach offers wide views across Herefordshire and leads to the summit of Black Hill. A peaty plateau leads to the source of the Olchon Brook, which breaks out of its boggy birthplace through a rocky escarpment known as Darren. The energetic watercourse quickly carves a romantic fertile valley, which is followed back to the starting point, a total of 5 miles.

START Black Hill picnic area and car park. SO 288328.

DIRECTIONS To reach this isolated spot, follow the minor road north from Longtown towards Llanveynoe past the castle. Continue until you pick up signs for the picnic area, directing you to the left.

*T*his is the second of two walks from Herefordshire. However for centuries this part of the county was a disputed area. Local place names are evidence of a distinctly Welsh lilt. The district was known in English as Archenfield and in Welsh as Ergyng depending on your preference. The Domesday Book refers to the disputed nature of the border marches. 'In Archenfield the king has three churches. The priests of these churches undertake the king's embassies into Wales, and each of them sings for the king two masses every week. When any one of them dies, the king customarily has 20s. from him. If any Welshman steals a man or a woman, a horse, an ox, or a cow, on being convicted, he first returns what has been stolen and [then] pays 20s. as a fine. If he kills any thegn's man, he gives 10s. to the lord of the slain man. But if a Welshman kills a Welshman, the relatives of the slain man come together and plunder the slayer and his kin and burn their houses until, toward noon on the following day, the body of the slain man is buried.' The phone box at Llanveynoe (in England) carries the title 'Teleffon', showing that BT is confused as well.

1 CROSS THE STILE from the car park giving access to the open hillside. Head directly and steeply up the ridge following the grass path between gorse bushes. The ascent is gentler once you have gained the crest. *It is a wonderful walk, giving a sense of freedom. In places the ridge, known locally as the Cat's Back, is less than six feet wide. But the path is broad and easy and views extend west across the Olchon Valley to the ridge marking the contemporary border. Eastwards there is a wide prospect over the Monnow Valley and across Herefordshire to the English Midlands. For much of its life the Monnow forms the border between England and Wales and gives its name to the town and county of Monmouth. However, it starts life as a Herefordshire stream rising firmly on the English side of the mountains. The stone castles that guard its banks at Longtown, Skenfrith and Monmouth illustrate its border credentials.* Soon after passing a wind shelter the ridge widens into a broad shoulder and you ascend gently to the summit of Black Hill, marked by a trig point at 640m.

2 From the trig point, BEAR LEFT and keep following the distinct path across rather boggy level moorland terrain. Follow the path for just under a mile. A small pile of stones on the path marks the junction with a bridleway. It could be easy to miss so watch out.

3 TURN SHARP LEFT to follow this route. It's a bridleway, though it's actually quite a narrow path. It soon begins to descend to a depression. Soon after a ruined shelter the depression is suddenly transformed into a steep sided valley and the stream descends a deep ravine. The Olchon Valley opens out in front of you and the path descends to the left of the stream. *It is rocky at first but then becomes a delightful grassy track among carpets of bilberry.*

4 Below a wood a gate gives access to a sunken lane, which can be rather muddy. But soon it joins a tarmac lane. Follow this in the same direction for about 1¼ miles. *It is extremely quiet, just serving farms at the head of the valley and the hedgerows and*

and religious conservatism. The tale gives insight into the struggle of border hill farmers in times past, not that it's an easy living today.

Offa's Dyke

*T*he Hatterrall ridge runs along the western edge of the Olchon valley and carries Offa's Dyke Long Distance Path. The path runs from Chepstow to Prestatyn, a length of 177 miles and was opened in 1971. Offa's Dyke is believed to date from the eighth century, built by Offa, king of Mercia, as a boundary marker and defensive earth-

views make it an attractive walk. Just across the valley lies Olchon Court. This is believed to be the site of one of the original Baptist churches from a time when non-conformists were persecuted. Its position on the remote border was deliberate. Believers were able to evade civil jurisdiction from either side. The congregation of farmers, shepherds and merchants could meet at night and move away quickly. The site probably predates the Reformation and the Baptist chapel may have been built on a sacred medieval foundation. When you come to a road junction, TURN LEFT following the sign to the picnic area. This soon brings you back to the starting point.

'On the Black Hill'

*B*lack Hill was the setting for the novel by Bruce Chatwin, 'On the Black Hill', which was made into a film in 1987. The moving story tells of twins who grow up together and spend all their lives in the hard graft of agricultural work on the land. For 80 years their lives are stifled by hardship, pride

work. At times it is a great earth bank, up to 25 feet high, accompanied by a deep ditch. In other places more modest features remain. There is little of the earthwork to be seen between Monmouth and Knighton, with just a few possible remains around Hereford. The route of the Dyke is a matter of speculation here. There is no evidence that it followed the Hatterrall ridge, but it makes a splendid route for the footpath. Parts of it are included in **Walks 4, 7** and **8** but the whole 17-mile section from Pandy to Hay can be walked in a day. (Take equipment for a long mountain walk, including a compass.)

TRETOWER, CEFN MOEL AND CWM CLARACH

DESCRIPTION A 7-mile tour of valley and mountain countryside, enjoying a wide variety of scenery and terrain. Starting from historic Tretower, the route crosses the Rhiangoll's flood plain to reach the site of a Roman fort. A climb up to the Cefn Moel ridge yields views over Llangorse Lake and the Brecon Beacons. The descent through a charming wooded valley brings you back to the river at Cwmdu, from where an old green road completes the circuit to Tretower.

START Tretower Court and Castle. SO 186213.

DIRECTIONS The village of Tretower is on the A479 between Crickhowell and Talgarth, a mile from its junction with the A40 at Nant-y-ffin. A lane leads from the A479 to Tretower Court. There is space to park at the roadside opposite the entrance.

*T*retower has always been at an important crossroads close to the confluence of the Usk and Rhiangoll. So perhaps it is unsurprising that there are two historic buildings on the same site here. The thirteenth century stone keep superseded an early Norman castle. Next to it is a rare example of a late medieval manor house. The present building dates from the fifteenth century. Both are in the care of Cadw and are open to the public (admission charge).

❙ WALK ALONG THE LANE by the church of St John the Evangelist. You pass the round tower and walls of Tretower castle on your left. *Some of the walls have been built into barns.* At the end of the village you pass another old chapel, now a house, on your right. Straight ahead is a gate with a public footpath sign to Gaer. GO THROUGH THE GATE and cross the field. At the far end a concrete bridge crosses the Rhiangoll and a

gate admits you to the next field. Keep to its right hand side next to a hedge. At the end pass through a gap and continue along the left hand edge of the next two fields, with a stile in the corner between them. At the end of the second field another stile gives access to a lane. TURN LEFT and follow the lane between two fences. Keep straight on past a group of houses including Lower Gaer Farm, where the lane becomes metalled. At the end of the lane come a T-junction and TURN RIGHT. Follow the lane as it weaves round and then climbs up Pen-y-gaer. *This is the site of a small Roman fort built half way along the Roman road from Brecon to Abergavenny.* Descend to another T-junction.

2 Immediately OPPOSITE THE JUNCTION CROSS A STILE that leads to an old lane almost overwhelmed by trees and undergrowth. To follow the right of way, climb two fields adjacent to this overgrown lane. At the top the second field, continue to follow its edge as it curves to the left. WATCH FOR A STILE in the hedge on the upper boundary. CROSS THIS AND CONTINUE UP the left hand edge of this final field. At the top a gate leads to a lane.

3 TURN RIGHT, pass a house and GO THROUGH A GATE THEN TURNING IMMEDIATELY LEFT up a green lane. Climb up this bridleway between trees and hedges alongside a small stream. At the top a gate leads to open land and a metalled road. CONTINUE STRAIGHT ACROSS THE ROAD and carry on up the wide track as it climbs through bracken and gorse, avoiding any deviations. After a while it levels out meets a wall on the crest of the ridge. KEEP THE WALL ON YOUR LEFT AND FOLLOW THE TRACK. *Soon you enjoy views left over Llangorse Lake.* Ignore any side turnings and keep on the main track. The wall gives way to a fence as you start a further gentle ascent, *topped by a small scar. 200 yards along the scar is the site of a prehistoric burial mound.* Soon after this there a slight descent leads to a major junction of paths marked by a small cairn right in the middle of the track and a group of larch trees 100 yards to your left.

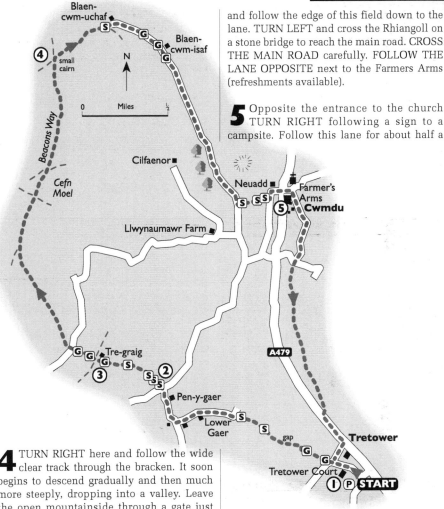

and follow the edge of this field down to the lane. TURN LEFT and cross the Rhiangoll on a stone bridge to reach the main road. CROSS THE MAIN ROAD carefully. FOLLOW THE LANE OPPOSITE next to the Farmers Arms (refreshments available).

5 Opposite the entrance to the church TURN RIGHT following a sign to a campsite. Follow this lane for about half a

4 TURN RIGHT here and follow the wide clear track through the bracken. It soon begins to descend gradually and then much more steeply, dropping into a valley. Leave the open mountainside through a gate just above Blaen-y-cwm-uchaf farm. A concrete track leads down the valley, accompanied by a stream. The lane passes through another farmyard and then continues, more level, along a charming valley with hedgerows of wild flowers and fields decorated with ash trees. After a while the lane descends again through thicker woodland. At the bottom of the hill CROSS A STILE ON THE LEFT marked with a Beacons Way sign. Follow the left hand side of the field as it crosses the bottom of the valley. *The village and church tower of Cwm Du lie ahead.* Just before the end of the field you cross a stile on the left

mile. Just past the campsite the lane turns sharp right down a hill. However you KEEP STRAIGHT ON here past the farm signs onto a green lane, an avenue between trees. *From this raised terrace on the side of the hill there are good views across the valley.* It continues for about a mile before joining the main road. TURN LEFT to walk along it. There is no alternative to 300 yards along the edge of this busy road. Take care, as there is no footpath. Just after the first house in the village TURN RIGHT down a very narrow lane. At the end of the lane TURN LEFT to return to Tretower Court.

21

Y DERI & THE SUGAR LOAF

DESCRIPTION A 5½-mile circular route that climbs one of the and most famous and distinctive of the Black Mountains. A gentle ascent through oak woodlands gives way to a splendid gorse covered ridge. The approach to the summit makes use of a spiral pathway that gives excellent all round views. Outstanding views and a sense of open space maintain interest throughout this classic conquest of one of the best-known Black Mountains.

START Llwyn Du car park SO 288167.

DIRECTIONS There is a small car park at Llwyn Du on the southern slopes of the Sugar Loaf. From Abergavenny town centre, follow the A40 towards Brecon for about ½ mile. Turn right, shortly before Neville Hall Hospital, to take Chapel Road. This rises northwards through residential areas and becomes a narrow lane as it leaves the town. It ends at a small car park at Llwyn Du. *Take a compass.*

1 Take the roughly surfaced lane continuing north from the car park. After a short way cross an old cattle grid and pass the National Trust sign to enter Parc Lodge. Continue on the track as it gently descends to cross the Afon Cibi. Shortly after, turn sharp RIGHT onto another forest track, now heading south on the opposite slope of the valley. Enjoy the oak woodlands, rich in birdsong, with the Afon Cibi gurgling down to your right.

2 By two cottages TURN SHARP LEFT and enter the National Trust's Y Deri land through a gate. *Almost all the Sugar Loaf is in the care of the National Trust, giving open access across wide and open countryside. On the south side, grassy spurs topped with springy turf, bracken and gorse, rise out of delightfully wooded valleys, giving a variety of excellent approaches to the mountain.*

This route uses one of these sylvan ascents to gain Y Deri ridge, following this to the summit. Climb steadily up a good track through the woods. Maintain this direction as the woods give way to more open bracken and gorse heath on the upper slopes. Pass a wall corner and soon reach the top of the ridge with prospects eastwards over the Skirrid (see **Walk 20**).

3 A good track leads northwards along the ridge. *The well-drained, springy turf makes for easy and pleasant walking and there are excellent views all around, with the Sugar Loaf now rising up to the left.* After just over a mile, you reach a gate with a track leading back into the Parc Lodge enclosure. Ignore this and keep outside the fence, following a path along its perimeter until you reach a junction with a small path to the RIGHT, leading directly towards the summit. There is a small holly tree on the left to confirm your navigation.

4 This track rises gently, and then more steeply as it approaches the summit. It is possible to make a beeline for the highest point, but it is far better to stick to the grassy path as it circumnavigates the upper cone of the mountain, like a turfed spiral staircase. *This is not only a gentler ascent, but also gives ever-changing views right round the mountain. First northwards over the Grwyne Fawr valley, then towards the bleak highest ground of the Black Mountains around Waun Fach (see Walks 5 and 17), then westwards up the Usk valley and finally south across Llanwenarth Common and Abergavenny to the Blorenge (see Walks 18 and 19). Shattered rocks mark the summit and the concise, shapely plateau is crowned by a trig point marking its height of 596m. The distinctive conical summit of the Sugar Loaf is a landmark for many miles around. Its profile can be made out from the Cotswold escarpment 50 miles to the east. The peak, known in Welsh as Pen y Fal, marks the gateway to the upper Usk valley, drawing the eye west into the hills and mountains of the interior of Wales.*

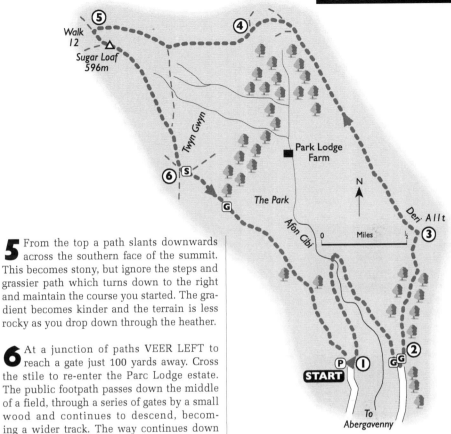

5 From the top a path slants downwards across the southern face of the summit. This becomes stony, but ignore the steps and grassier path which turns down to the right and maintain the course you started. The gradient becomes kinder and the terrain is less rocky as you drop down through the heather.

6 At a junction of paths VEER LEFT to reach a gate just 100 yards away. Cross the stile to re-enter the Parc Lodge estate. The public footpath passes down the middle of a field, through a series of gates by a small wood and continues to descend, becoming a wider track. The way continues down through a succession of fields, dotted with mature trees and leads you back to the car park at Llwyn Du.

Sugar Loaf

WALK 12

CWM GWENFFRWD & THE SUGAR LOAF

DESCRIPTION This 5½–mile walk approaches the Sugar Loaf from the west. You can climb directly from Llangenny but parking is not easy there. So this route starts from the excellent car park on Llanwenarth Common. Instead of the well-trodden direct ascent, the walk makes use of a good network of tracks around the wooded shoulder of the mountain. After crossing Cwm Gwenffrwd, a pleasant ridge path leads onto the spur of Mynydd Pen-y-fal before striking out directly for the summit of the mountain.

START Car Park on Llanwenarth Common. SO 267167.

DIRECTIONS A narrow lane leaves the A40 on the western outskirts of Abergavenny. Signs to Sugar Loaf Vineyard point you in the right direction. Pass the vineyard to continue climbing up the slopes of the Sugar Loaf. After a while the lane turns west and climbs around the side of the mountain to reach a good car park. This is an excellent viewpoint over the Usk valley and the Brecon Beacons. It also offers a bird's eye view of Abergavenny. Identification of features is aided by a toposcope. *Take a compass.*

From the car park continue along the tarmac lane westwards. *Enjoy extensive views across the Usk valley to Gilwern and the Clydach Gorge. This narrow valley carries the main road up to the 'heads of the valleys' en route to Merthyr and Swansea. Two hundred years ago it was a hive of industrial activity and a centre for iron making. Today old tramways and abandoned limestone quarries invite careful exploration, and this environment has proved a fertile ground for plants in the nature reserve situated here.* The lane bends past Llyweddrog Farm and continues to meander through a series of fields studded with a variety of trees. After a while you pass a series of farm buildings at Pen-y-graig.

2 Just beyond these you come to a T-junction and TURN RIGHT. Holly and hazel bushes form an avenue for the lane as it passes across fields and then descends through a wood. Go straight across a junction of tracks and continue past the house at Cwm-cegyr. Curve round to cross the stream. Pass through a gate. *This is Cwm Gwenffrwd, a charming wooded valley. The echo of bird-song mingles with the gentle babbling of the brook as it carries water from the Sugar Loaf down to the Grwyne and the Usk.*

3 About 200 yards beyond the gate TURN SHARP RIGHT up a track signposted to 'The Hill'. The path emerges from the woods to curve to the right, ascending a field with a fence on the left, now heading straight for the Sugar Loaf. *A lovely variety of trees graces the far bank of the stream.* At the top of the field cross a stile next to a gate and continue on the bridleway. Soon a gate gives access to the open hillside.

4 Just before you cross the stream TURN SHARP LEFT to ascend a grassy track slanting up through the bracken. *As it levels out it curves round to the right opening up the prospect of the highest tops of the Black Mountains, the Usk valley and the Brecon Beacons.* On the brow of the hill, opposite a gate giving access to a bridleway, TURN RIGHT to follow a path climbing the crest of the ridge. As you gain the top of the ridge you join another path coming up from the left and CURVE RIGHT for a direct assault on the summit. A straightforward grassy track leads inexorably to the shattered rocks of summit cone. The highest point is marked with a trig point at 596m. *The view from here takes in the Black Mountains to the north, the Brecon Beacons to the west and the edge of the South Wales iron and coal belt to the south. The strategic position of Abergavenny is evident to the south-east, guarding the entrance to the upper Usk valley and the route through to West Wales. Here was the Roman fort of Gobannium. The remains of a Norman castle offers evidence of its importance in later centuries. During the industrial revolution it was a garrison town, with soldiers used to subdue the vola-*

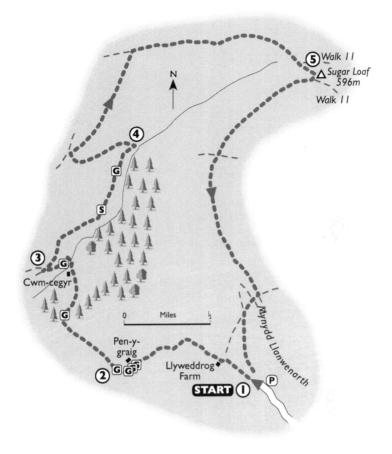

tility of the nearby industrial towns, when the need arose.

5 To return from the summit DESCEND BY THE TRACK that heads west-south-west (*240 degrees*) from the summit. In mist you will need a compass to confirm your direction, though the path is unmistakeable once you've found it. After a stony start it soon becomes a wide grassy passageway that descends gracefully down the mountain, gradually curving around the head of Cwm Trosnant. *The lower south-facing slopes of the mountain offer protection from the harshest weather. Vines have been grown here and* in other nearby spots in recent years. At a crossing of paths above the cwm you TURN RIGHT to follow another grassy track curving gently down to the car park.

ALTERNATIVE DIRECT ASCENT

If you're short of time, the direct descent could be used for the outward climb as well. It makes a straightforward and easy walk, mostly on well-drained, grassy tracks. But, remember, the Sugar Loaf's summit is over 2,000 feet above sea level and you should be prepared for unexpected weather.

CWM IAU & HATTERRALL HILL

DESCRIPTION Ancient oak woodland, riverside meadows, an isolated valley and the heather-clad moorland of the border ridge combine to make this a varied and interesting expedition around the south eastern fringe of the Black Mountains.

START Llanfihangel Crucorney SO 326207.

DIRECTIONS Llanfihangel village is just off the A465 about 5 miles north of Abergavenny. The bus service between Hereford and Abergavenny stops at the Skirrid Inn in the village. Roadside parking is available.

From the road junction in the centre of the village, walk northwards along the road towards Llanthony for about 300 yards. It soon comes to another junction next to the river at Pen-y-bont. TURN RIGHT at the sign to Longtown and cross the bridge. Immediately after the house on the far side of the bridge, TURN LEFT over a stile at a footpath sign to Hatterrall Hill. Follow the path, now also the line of the Beacons Way, along the left hand side of the field. Cross the railway, taking particular care as this is a fast and busy main line and visibility is restricted because of bends in the track. Continue to follow the route up through the fields to the buildings at Great Llwygy. In front of the house, TURN LEFT and take the track, still the Beacons Way, climbing diagonally through the woods, soon passing a mobile phone mast on the left. It emerges on to a small area of heath land at the top of the hill and a grand panorama lies at your feet. Below is the Honddu valley and beyond are the highest ridges of the Black Mountains. Hatterrall Hill, our ultimate destination today, looms up to the right. The track becomes a grassy path and bends right over the top of the hill, then descending to a gate and stile. Leave the Beacons Way here and TURN LEFT to follow the track

towards a house. After the next gate, don't turn right on the track down to the house. Instead, descend the field diagonally, passing above the house. Cross a stile and drop steeply down the next field to a gate into woodland. As you go through the gate you enter Strawberry Wood Nature Reserve, a small area of ancient oak woodland, managed by the Gwent Wildlife Trust. The path leads down through the reserve to arrive near a house, Strawberry Cottage, where a display board gives further information. Just before the house, TURN SHARP RIGHT and follow the path along the riverside. Ignore the footbridge and continue along the edge of the field to a stile at the far end. The route traverses a couple more waterside meadows before joining a small road. *At this point it is a short distance along the road to the left to reach the Queen's Arms, where food and drink are available. This is also an alternative starting point for this walk and Walk 14. A small charge is payable for parking.*

2 To continue on the walk, cross the lane, mount a stile, and follow the right of way across another riverside meadow. At the far end, your way crosses another stile and turns gently uphill, through a surprisingly boggy field, to reach the lane once more. TURN LEFT and follow the narrow and very quiet road to a junction about ⅓ mile further on. The road to the left leads to the village of Cwmyoy with its remarkable crooked church and landslip. BEAR RIGHT here and walk along the cul de sac as it climbs along the bottom of Cwm Iau, a quiet side valley of the Honddu, engulfed by the high ridges on either side.

3 At the head of the cwm, the way leads through the farm buildings at Blaenyoy and on to a grassy track, which weaves its way up the hillside. At first the route is very clear and distinct, but as you near the top of the ridge, among the heather and bracken, the way becomes less clear. Veer right at a suitable point and cross the heather on to the top of the ridge. This is all open access land. You will not miss the broad track marking the line of the long distance footpath from Prestatyn to Chepstow, which is also

4 The track continues south over the top of Hatterrall Hill, marked by a trig point. The distinctive profile of Ysgyryd Fawr (The Skirrid) lies straight ahead, as though guarding the approach to Abergavenny. Follow the Offa's Dyke path route where it bears left off the main track and carry on down through heather and bracken, ignoring the Beacons Way where this turns off to the right. Eventually you arrive at a gate, leading to a sunken lane and, shortly, on to a road. TURN RIGHT and follow this lane to a cross roads in around ⅓ mile. TURN LEFT, still on the route of the Offa's Dyke 'path'. About ¼ mile later, the road bends right by a house. Just past the house, BEAR LEFT across a stile and follow the path diagonally down the next field to re-emerge on to the road. TURN LEFT and follow the road down to a T junction.

5 At the junction, carry on STRAIGHT AHEAD over a stile and shortly cross the railway line and then a footbridge over the river. The path leads along the left hand side of the field to the main road. TURN LEFT along the main road for about 200 yards before crossing a stile to the LEFT. Follow the path across

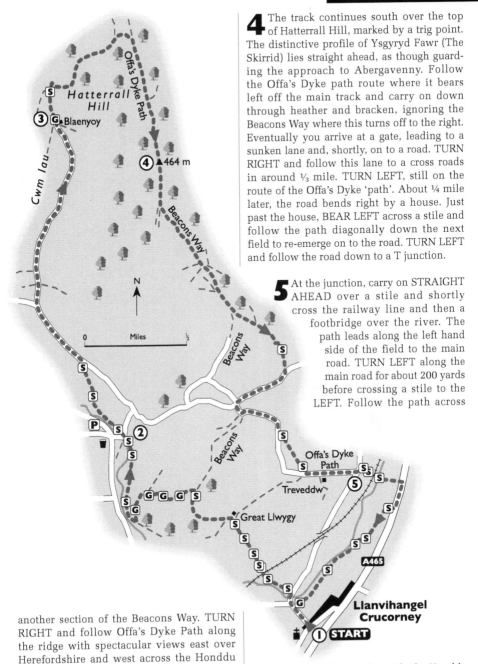

another section of the Beacons Way. TURN RIGHT and follow Offa's Dyke Path along the ridge with spectacular views east over Herefordshire and west across the Honddu Valley and over the Black Mountains. This is the border between Wales and England and it makes a particularly dramatic frontier.

the next field and then alongside the Honddu back to Pen-y-bont. At the gate TURN LEFT and climb the short hill back to Llanfihangel.

27

WALK 14

AROUND TWYN-Y-GAER

DESCRIPTION This is an enjoyable 5-mile saunter with much of historical interest. From the car park a steady ascent leads to a wooded promenade along the southern side of the Vale of Ewyas. An Iron Age fort caps the summit of Twyn-y-Gaer with panoramic views over three valleys. A shady lane leads down from the common with westward views across the Grwyne Fawr valley while the return route follows a high level green road, commanding views of Cwm Coed-y-Cerrig and the Sugar Loaf.

START Walkers' Car Park just north of the Queen's Head Inn. SO 311222.

DIRECTIONS The Queen's Head Inn is situated 1½ miles along the Llanthony road from its junction with the A465 at Llanfihangel Crucorney. The Walkers' Car Park is on the opposite side of the road. A small charge is requested and should be paid at the pub.

1 Ascend the steep tarmac lane, which leaves the valley road at the entrance to the car park. A steady climb leads through the woods up the ridge of Twyn-y-Gaer. Eventually the tarmac ends and the ascent gives way to a level promenade. *This is a charming, easy walk and through the trees you can survey the Vale of Ewyas below. The prospect includes the crooked church and landslip at Cwmyoy on the other side of the valley. A little further along the steep cliffs of Darren rise abruptly to the high moorland and the English border.*

2 Pass through a gate to enter the open land. Immediately TURN LEFT and climb up a broad grassy track through the bracken. It veers to the left just below the highest part of the hill and then attacks the summit from the east. A cairn marks the top at 427m. *The summit plateau is a delightful grassy promenade, studded with gorse bushes. It's easy to see why the ancient Britons chose this site, perched on a hilltop overlooking three valleys. The ditches and ramparts*

are still discernable. The fort is oval in shape and covers an area of over 4 acres. It consists of three sections, surrounded by a double embankment. From the top you can see the sites of two neighbouring forts. Eastwards lies Trewyn at the southern end of the Hatterrall ridge, while Crug Hywel crowns the Table Mountain above Crickhowell (see Walk 16). At the top carry STRAIGHT ON past the cairn to the end of the summit plateau. A deep defensive ditch marks the boundary of the fort. It is easiest to cross this at the left hand end, then picking up a clear grassy path SLOPING DOWNHILL TO THE RIGHT. After a short steep section, there's a graceful descent through the bracken to the wide saddle of the ridge. *From here you can see the ridge ahead is quite narrow and the valleys either side are not far apart. But they drain in completely different directions. To the left, the Grwyne Fawr's waters supply the Usk, eventually passing under Newport's transporter bridge to join the Bristol Channel. To the left the Honddu unites with the Monnow a few miles north, and the water then flows to the Wye and on to the Severn at Chepstow.*

3 At the bottom you come to a wall and meet a track running alongside it. BEAR LEFT to join this track and continue along it. In about 500 yards you pass a house set back on the right. About 300 yards further you reach a junction of tracks.

4 TURN SHARP LEFT here, doubling back to a southerly direction. Follow this lane just above a wall and a wood and just below the crest of the ridge.

5 Close to a ruined hut another track leads downhill sharply to the right. *To join up with **Walk 6** to Patrishow and the Grwyne Valley, turn right and follow this bridleway downhill for 500 yards, reaching the farmhouse at Ty Mawr.* To stay on this walk, ignore the turning and carry STRAIGHT ON keeping to the green lane, which is now enclosed. A gate leads to a walled lane, which descends gradually with views across the Grwyne Fawr and over to the Sugar Loaf (*See Walks 11 and 12*). Towards the bottom, the lane is joined by a concrete track from

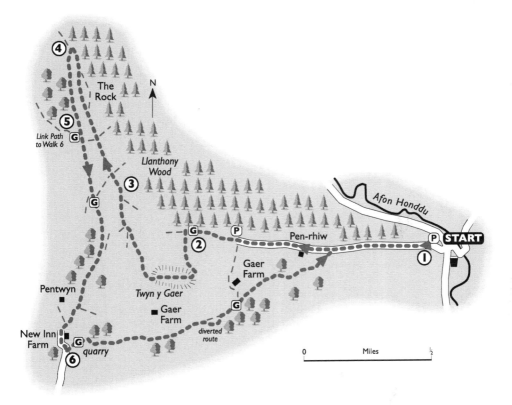

the left and becomes roughly surfaced as it approaches some farm buildings. Follow the road past New Inn Farm and the white-washed cottages.

6 Just below the farm and next to a telegraph pole, TURN SHARP LEFT to follow a lane, which may be muddy here, and pass through a gate. Avoid side turnings to a quarry and ascend steadily on the track through oak, holly and hazel trees. *As the lane levels out enjoy south facing views over Cwm Coed-y-Cerrig and the National Nature Reserve, managed by the Countryside Council for Wales. The boggy area in the bottom of the valley includes many alder trees and offers a good habitat for frogs. Higher up the hillside, towards the course of our walk, drier terrain supports mixed woodland including oak, ash, beech and hazel. The secretive Dormouse can*

be found here, so look out! If you want to visit the reserve itself, the car park can be reached by way of the road towards Forest Coalpit. On the highest section of the route a cinder track provides a sensible a diversion around a house. A gate leads to a walled lane, which descends through the trees and joins your outward route. TURN RIGHT to walk down the lane to the car park.

Twyn-y-gaer

T *he local Silures tribe fought the Romans from the hill fort at Twyn-y-Gaer. More evidence of a turbulent past is found a little further along the ridge to the north of this walk. The Revenge Stone, Y Ddial Garreg, commemorates the spot where local Welsh tenants struck back at a tyrannical Norman overlord (SO 284243).*

MYNYDD LLYSIAU & THE GRWYNE FECHAN

DESCRIPTION This is a delightful but energetic 9½-mile excursion into one of the remotest recesses of the Black Mountains. The outward leg climbs from the foot of Cwm Banw. Once the modest climb to Tal Trwymau is complete you have the prospect of a gentle ridge walk with superb views all the way to the isolated mountain pass at the head of the Grwyne Fechan valley. From here the return route makes use of a clear and well-graded path known as Macnamara's road. It skirts the wild hillside before crossing the river at Tal-y-maes Bridge. The lower reaches are adorned by woodland before a final lane walk offers lush hedgerows decked in wild flowers. *Moutain precautions are needed.*

START A small parking area just next to a bridge at Cwm Banw, in the Grwyne Fechan valley. SO 234229

DIRECTIONS From Crickhowell, a minor road leads north from the A40 and into the Grwyne Fechan valley. Just after a sharp bend and a bridge, there is a small parking area by the road. There is enough space for about five cars.

1 Cross the stile next to the parking area and BEAR RIGHT to follow a permissive path up hill using marker posts as a guide. At the top of the field go through a gateway and TURN LEFT up an enclosed track following a sign, 'To the Mountain'. After a while go through another gate and keep to the main track ascending up the ridge with a wall on your left. *Views now open up ahead to the top of the Grwyne Fechan valley and beyond. Small conifer plantations and bracken add colour to the hillside. To the left the view lies across Cwm Banw to the limestone massif of Pen Cerrig-calch (See Walk 16).* Climb past a plantation then cross a stile. Keep to the main track as it ascends to a substantial cairn on the crest of the ridge. From here a broad grassy path ascends gently along the broad ridge past some old quarry workings. A pleasant, easy walk follows a distinct route and offers excellent views with the bulk of Pen Allt-mawr now dominating the western outlook. The ridge swells to the summit of Pen Twyn Glas. *Now views north encompass the Rhiangoll valley and Mynydd Troed. To the south-west, the distinctive profile of the Brecon Beacons presides over the horizon.*

2 At Pen Twyn Glas KEEP STRAIGHT AHEAD along a narrow but clear path across a rather soggy saddle. Soon a boundary stone crowns the top of a small knoll. Continue past this following the broad path slightly left leading towards the top of Mynydd Llysiau. You could be forgiven for missing the summit, a negligible swelling marked only by a few stones. But this is a minor defect in a mountain with such a grand prospect. *The view north is magnificent. The proud form of Mynydd Troed (See Walk 19) does bear resemblance to the profile of a foot, as its Welsh name implies. You can see the ancient site of Castell Dinas guarding the head of the Rhiangoll valley (see Walk 5) and beyond the Wye Valley towards Builth and Hay. A short but steep descent now leads to a high mountain pass. This is an important junction of six mountain paths, at an isolated spot 618m above sea level. To the sharp left a well-engineered route leads into Cwm Nant-yr-ychen. Another route bears left and soon splits into two. Both these lead to the upper reaches of the Rhiangoll valley. One takes the contoured descent along Rhiw Trumau followed on Walk 5. The path straight ahead climbs the steep ridge to Pen Trumau and on to Waun Fach, the highest peak in the Black Mountains. This major junction and neat pass is unnamed on maps but it deserves a title. Bwlch Trumau might be a suitable description. In front of you lies the very head of the Grwyne Fechan, spawned by drainage down the extensive flank of Waun Fach. A myriad of boggy springs combine to give birth to the infant river whose waters have driven a deep trench southwards through the hills.*

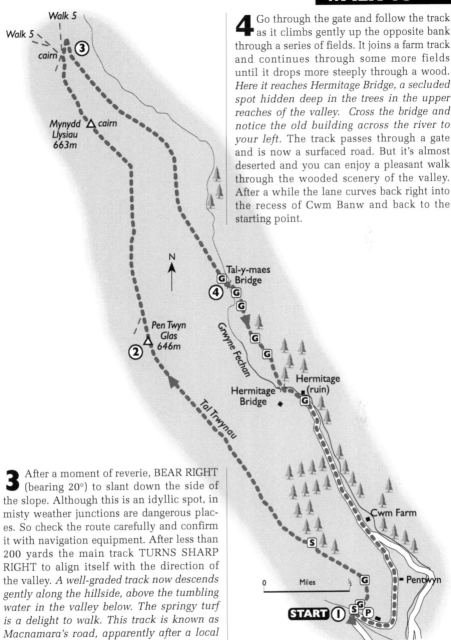

4 Go through the gate and follow the track as it climbs gently up the opposite bank through a series of fields. It joins a farm track and continues through some more fields until it drops more steeply through a wood. *Here it reaches Hermitage Bridge, a secluded spot hidden deep in the trees in the upper reaches of the valley. Cross the bridge and notice the old building across the river to your left.* The track passes through a gate and is now a surfaced road. But it's almost deserted and you can enjoy a pleasant walk through the wooded scenery of the valley. After a while the lane curves back right into the recess of Cwm Banw and back to the starting point.

3 After a moment of reverie, BEAR RIGHT (bearing 20°) to slant down the side of the slope. Although this is an idyllic spot, in misty weather junctions are dangerous places. So check the route carefully and confirm it with navigation equipment. After less than 200 yards the main track TURNS SHARP RIGHT to align itself with the direction of the valley. *A well-graded track now descends gently along the hillside, above the tumbling water in the valley below. The springy turf is a delight to walk.* This track is known as Macnamara's road, apparently after a local eighteenth century landowner who used it to visit his mistress. *Lower down a conifer plantation decorates the opposite hillside.* The track eventually leads down to the river and crosses it at Tal-y-maes Bridge.

TABLE MOUNTAIN & PEN CERRIG-CALCH

DESCRIPTION This 6-mile walk climbs from the centre of Crickhowell to the flat-topped summit of Table Mountain, crowned with an Iron Age fort. It rises north of the town, which derives its name from the fort's Welsh title of Crug Hywel. Beyond Table Mountain a further climb leads to the limestone dome of Pen Cerrig-calch, at 701m the highest point of the walk. The return route retraces steps to Table Mountain before following an alternative path down a wooded valley into the town. A suggestion for a 10 mile linear ridge walk is included at the end.

START The main car park in Crickhowell. SO 218184.

DIRECTIONS Crickhowell lies astride the A40, about 7 miles from Abergavenny and 13 miles from Brecon. The pay-and-display car park is signposted from the A40 in the centre of the town.

I *Crickhowell is an attractive town, marinated in history. A Norman castle, a fine bridge across the Usk and the fourteenth century parish church are just some of the features that give Crickhowell an air of permanence.* Walk through the town following the main road towards Brecon. Just after a petrol station, TURN RIGHT up Llanbedr Road. At the end of the houses it becomes a narrow lane. At the junction with Great Oak Road KEEP LEFT with Table Mountain rising straight ahead. Opposite an electricity sub station, TURN LEFT through a gate and follow a walled lane, a public footpath. A small reservoir is passed on the right with a plaque expressing gratitude for its gift. At the top of the lane cross the stile into the farmyard and TURN RIGHT in front of the house. Pass though a gate and walk across the field with the hedge on your left. At the end of the field another gate leads to a footpath enclosed between two hedges. TURN LEFT and follow the path. At the top a stile leads into a field. Climb up the right hand side of the next two fields. Then a stile leads on to a farm track. TURN LEFT and follow the track as it turns up hill through a gateway and stile into a field. The track ends here but the path continues up the right hand side of this field next to the hedge. At the top of the field, cross a stile and TURN RIGHT, following the footpath as it climbs up through the woods above a house. At the top of the wood, a stile gives access to the open hillside. The summit of the Table Mountain lies up to the left and a path leads steeply through the bracken to gain the rocky plateau.

2 *The summit would make a very lop-sided table. The plateau slopes from north to south but was an excellent vantage point for the Iron Age people who built a fort here. The location became known as Crug Hywel, the fort of Hywel Dda, Hywel the Good. Hywel was a tenth century leader, chiefly remembered for instituting a code of law, which did much to unify the country.* From the top, descend the northern flank across the remains of the defensive ditch and gain the saddle of land just below the rocky summit. From the saddle you could shorten the walk by following the return route directly from here (see instructions from Point 4). Otherwise, follow the broad path across the saddle and on up the slopes of the Pen Cerrig-calch. As you climb, bracken gives way to gorse. The main path curves helpfully around the steeper rocky section at Trwyn Ysgwrfa. It is much more pleasant to follow this than the direct short cut. At the top of the steep section a steady but gentler ascent heads towards a cairn on the skyline. This is not the top but does mark the point where the path gains the summit area. From the cairn a short walk through shattered rocks leads to the trig point and a nearby wind shelter.

3 *Pen Cerrig-calch means 'limestone peak'. It is unique in the Black Mountains, which are almost all made of sandstone. It is probably an outlier of the limestone ridge rising on the south side of the Usk Valley opposite, around Mynydd Llangynidr. From* here retrace steps to the saddle below the summit of the Table Mountain, unless you want to carry on along the ridge (see note on a long distance traverse below).

4 At the saddle, instead of climbing the last few yards to the top of Table Mountain, TURN RIGHT to follow a path through the bracken, which weaves a route just above the boundary of enclosed land below. Eventually it descends more steeply to some ruins then a small copse of mature trees.

5 It leaves open country through a couple of sheepfolds before going through a gate into a walled lane. The lane is shared with a small stream for a while but stepping-stones ease the way towards a lovely field surrounded by a variety of trees. The route follows the left hand side of the field, crossing a small stream to a gate in the corner. This leads to a lane descending through woodland. The stream soon accompanies you through the glade. Beyond a further gate, there are views across Crickhowell. At the point where the lane bends left through a gate, leave it in favour of a stile marked with a footpath sign. Follow this path down through the fields to the houses of Crickhowell. At the bottom a sign guides you through the houses, past a school, to the A40. Follow this LEFT to return to the start.

A LONG DISTANCE TRAVERSE

If you can arrange transport, Crickhowell makes a good starting point for a 10-mile linear traverse of the western side of the Black Mountains. This offers spectacular views and a sense of space and freedom. This continues from Pen Cerrig-calch to follow a high level

ridge walk taking in four 2,000 foot peaks before dropping to the important pass at Pengenffordd, close to Wales' highest castle. **This is a serious mountain exploration.**

Follow directions for Walk 16 until Point 3, the summit of Pen Cerrig-calch. Instead of returning from here, CONTINUE ALONG THE PATH THAT HEADS NORTH-WEST along the ridge. After 3/4 mile it veers north and a gentle ascent leads to the summit of Pen Allt-mawr at 719m. The path then descends more steeply from the summit to pass around the head of Cwm Banw and on to Pen Twyn Glas. At Pen Twyn Glas KEEP STRAIGHT AHEAD along a narrow but clear path across a rather soggy saddle. Soon a boundary stone crowns the top of a small knoll. Continue past this following the broad path slightly left leading towards the top of Mynydd Llysiau. *For more details of this section, see Walk 15, point 2.* A short but steep descent now leads to a high mountain pass, marked by a cairn and the junction of six mountain routes.

At the cairn BEAR LEFT (bearing 300 degrees). The track slants down across the hillside and in about 200 yards be careful to follow the main path as it BEARS LEFT to descend directly down the mountain. *The final section is described in Walk 5 (from Point 6).* This brings you to the Castle Inn at Pengenffordd, at the highest point on the Crickhowell to Talgarth road.

Map labels:

Long-distance traverse to Pengenffordd

3 Pen Cerrig-calch 701m

Trwyn Ysgwrfa

Butts

4 Saddle

5

Table Mountain

2

Crug Hywel Fort

Cwm Cumbeth

Ysgubor-newydd

N

G G

G

A40

Crickhowell

A4077 **1 START** **i P**

0 Miles 1/2

WALK 17

THE WILD HEIGHTS OF THE BLACK MOUNTAINS

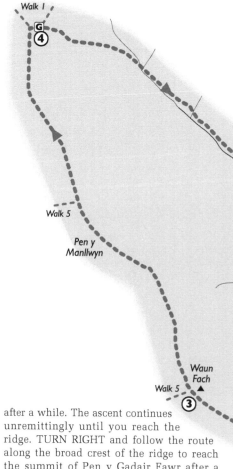

DESCRIPTION An adventurous 9 mile circuit that includes the two highest summits in the Black Mountains. Starting from a remote and idyllic forest car park, the outward route climbs steadily up to the ridge, gaining the top of Pen y Gadair Fawr. A long section of easy, though soggy, ridge walking crosses two other 2,000 foot peaks, including Waun Fach, the highest point in the Black Mountains. The return route follows an ancient track alongside the highest reaches of the Grwyne Fawr. *Care is needed with navigation in misty weather.*

START Forestry Commission car park at Mynydd Du. SO 253285

DIRECTIONS The car park is close to the end of the lane up the Grwyne Fawr valley. This is a long cul-de-sac, which starts at the crossroads at Forest Coalpit and follows the river northwards deep into the heart of the Black Mountains. Forest Coalpit can be accessed by narrow lanes from Crickhowell or by leaving the A465 at Llanfihangel Crucorney, four miles north of Abergavenny.

Follow the path from the far end of the car park. This soon leads back on to the valley road. Continue along this lane with a grassy clearing beside the river and conifer plantations rising up on each side. After ¼ mile, leave the lane to cross a wooden footbridge over the river to the LEFT. Once on the far bank, TURN RIGHT and follow a small but clear path along the river bank. After a short distance a stile leads out of the woods. TURN LEFT and climb a steep path up the left hand side of a gully. This continues to rise with the forest on the left and the gully on your right. The path can be muddy and slippery and at times there is a steep drop down to the stream. But the route is always clear and the gradient eases

after a while. The ascent continues unremittingly until you reach the ridge. TURN RIGHT and follow the route along the broad crest of the ridge to reach the summit of Pen y Gadair Fawr after a short distance. *Pen y Gadair Fawr is crowned by a cairn and, at 800 metres (2625 feet) is the second highest summit in the Black Mountains. Although 10 metres lower than Waun Fach, it is a more distinct elevation and, from here, you can see the other six peaks that rise above 2000 feet in the Black Mountains. On this ridge these include Pen Twyn Mawr to the south (2159 feet), and Waun Fach (2657 feet) to the north west. The other four 'Corbetts' are strung along the ridge to the west, across the valley of the Grwyne Fechan. From the south these include Pen Cerrig–calch (2300 feet), Pen Allt–mawr (2359 feet), Pen Twyn Glas (2119 feet) and finally Mynydd Llysiau (2175 feet). (See Walk 16 and its extension for details).*

2 Continue along the broad ridge in a north westerly direction. Although there is an intermittent path, the route is boggy in places as it crosses the soggy saddle of the ridge. You will need to take care in misty weather and use a compass or GPS to confirm your route. After just over a mile you reach the summit of Waun Fach, the highest point of the Black Mountains, though hardly its most dramatic focus. *The OS trig point has long since disappeared, perhaps swallowed up in the voracious black mud that engulfs the summit. The distant views compensate for the immediate miry swamp. You can see from Exmoor to the Cotswold escarpment, not to mention much of southern Wales. On a clear day, of course!*

which can be traversed almost without noticing. After a while the route begins to descend gradually until it reaches a saddle and junction of paths. This is the end of the mountain range and a new world opens up ahead as the dramatic northern sandstone escarpment of the Mynyddoedd Duon drops sharply into the fertile farming land of the Wye Valley. Mid Wales beckons beyond.

4 But this walk lurches back to the south east at this point, preferring the wild moorland to the tamed lowlands. TURN RIGHT here to follow the broad track towards Grwyne Fawr reservoir. This was an old road that crossed the Black Mountains. It is now a rough bridleway offering an atmospheric and wild crossing through the mountains, also popular with cyclists. The track gently drops through the damp gestating grounds of the Grwyne Fawr. The way itself is mostly firm, if eroded, and soon carves its way between the long ridges on either side. After about a mile and a half the Grwyne Fawr reservoir appears down to the left. *This was completed in 1928. It was built to provide water for the area around Abertillery in Monmouthshire's western valley, now Blaenau Gwent. A temporary town, Blaen-y-cwm, was built to house the workers. The track continues above and beyond the reservoir. In the valley below*

Grwyne Fawr Reservoir

Grwyne Fawr

Pen y Gadair Fawr ②

START P ①

3 The route beyond Waun Fach continues to follow the broad ridge in a north-north westerly direction. To the left the ridge drops more steeply into the infant reaches of the Rhiangoll valley. A modest squelchy elevation marks the summit of Pen y Manllwyn,

the dam, you can trace the access road that serves it. The road up the Grwyne Valley was only built in 1912 as part of the construction project. Eventually, it drops across the hillside to re-join the road just before the car park and our starting point.

CUSOP DINGLE & HAY BLUFF

DESCRIPTION Hay is a historic and attractive border town on the banks of the Wye. In 1961 Richard Booth started trading books in Hay. Today it is well known for its panoply of second hand bookshops crammed into a network of small streets. It is also home to Hay Literary Festival, which takes place around the spring bank holiday each year. This 9 mile walk climbs out of Hay through the picturesque wooded cleft of Cusop Dingle. It climbs on to the dramatic northern escarpment of the Black Mountains, with an optional 2 mile extension to the summit of Hay Bluff. The return route follows the line of Offa's Dyke long distance path.

START Main car park, Hay-on-Wye. SO 230422.

DIRECTIONS Hay lies 2 miles off the A438 Hereford-Brecon road and sits just on the Welsh side of the border. There is a regular bus service from both Hereford and Brecon.

1 From the car park, TURN RIGHT and follow Oxford Road around a double bend. Cross the stream and the border into England. On the far side of the bridge, TURN RIGHT along a lane at a sign to Cusop Dingle. This quiet cul de sac takes you up through the village of Cusop and alongside Dulas Brook. The buildings become more intermittent and the damp, steep sides of Cusop Dingle are clad with hart's tongue fern. A series of former mills bear witness to past industrial use of the fast flowing water as it carves a passage through red sandstone.

2 The paved road ends by a sign for 'Brickyard Cottage'. Ignore the right hand fork and carry STRAIGHT ON following a footpath sign past a white house on the right. Continue over a stile on to a track, crossing a field and entering a wood. At first the route accompanies the stream, muddy at times, but then slants up the hillside away from the valley bottom until it reaches a disused quarry. The path now narrows but continues to climb above the stream which cascades down a gully through a series of waterfalls. After a slight descent, cross the stream. Then veer sharply RIGHT on the opposite bank to reach a stile above. Once over the stile there is no clear path but a waymark points the direction along the bottom of the field just above the trees. Level at first, the route then curves up to the left, following the line of the stream below. Aim for a house on the hillside ahead, ignoring a track crossing the stream below it. At the top, reach a stile in front of a shed. Cross this and TURN RIGHT along the track which now passes above the houses. The path continues, more or less level, along the hillside. After a slight drop come to a junction of tracks. TURN SHARP RIGHT here and follow this to a stile which yields to a tarmac drive way. Walk along this down to a ford and footbridge. On the other side, the lane climbs up past a builder's yard to a road.

3 TURN LEFT and follow this quiet road for just over ¼ mile. At the point where it doubles back over the stream, leave the road and carry STRAIGHT AHEAD over a stile on to a track. But don't get too attached to this; it doesn't lead far! Instead, after 50 yards, look for some steps carved into the bank on the LEFT, indicated with a yellow arrow. Leave the track here and follow the right of way (not always evident as a path) as it climbs to the left of a small patch of scrubby woodland and on up the crest of a small ridge between two valleys. The route is on short, cropped turf and the full profile of Hay Bluff lies directly ahead.

4 When you reach the top, a wall and fence block your way on to the bridleway beyond. To reach this legally, go through a gate in the fence to the left, just below the top. Cross the corner of the next field and come to a stile at the top edge. Mount this and TURN RIGHT along the bridleway. The track is boggy at first but another gate leads on to a drier section. Soon after the gate cross a small stream which marks the return into Wales. Follow the track as it climbs gradually through the middle of bracken and gorse, rather than following the lower line of the fence. It's an exhilarating traverse of open hillside. Dropping to another small stream, come to a junction and here join Offa's Dyke Path swooping down from the ridge. BEAR RIGHT and follow the path through the bracken to the road - the mountain route across the Gospel Pass. The rest of the walk takes the route of the long distance footpath so the national trail acorn markers aid navigation. *From this point you can climb to the top of Hay Bluff if you want to extend the walk. To do so, TURN LEFT along the road to a parking area. From here a footpath leads directly up the escarpment and then climbs up to the plateau itself. This is actually an alternative route for Offa's Dyke Path. Although it's not far, adding less than two miles for the round trip, there is an extra 800 feet of climbing and the summit of Hay Bluff is wild moorland over 2,000 feet above sea level. So if you're going to attempt it, be prepared.*

5 TURN RIGHT along the road. Look out for an embedded boulder with an arrow and national trail marker on the left. At this point leave the road and BEAR LEFT to follow the line of Offa's Dyke footpath across the wide open pasture aiming for the top of a small rise. Occasional waymarked boulders guide your way to this and beyond. Nearly a mile after leaving the road, you are funnelled into a muddy hollow at the end of the open country and, at the end, pass through a gate on to a sunken lane. Beyond some farm buildings the lane becomes surfaced. Just before a gate, watch out for a stile on the RIGHT marked with a footpath symbol. Leave the lane and cross the stile. The path drops steeply down through fields and woodland to reach the Hay to Llanthony road once again. Follow this LEFT for a few yards before a stile on the RIGHT takes the path into a field. Follow the edge of this above a small valley and on round to the left, now above Cusop and the outward route. The last section passes a succession of fields and gates. The route is clear enough and soon emerges right next to the recycling bins at Hay's main car park.

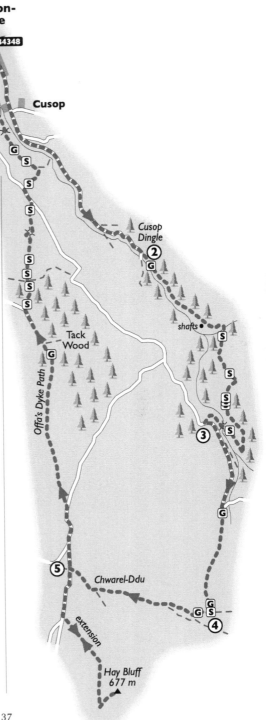

MYNYDD TROED & MYNYDD LLANGORSE

DESCRIPTION Two great tracts of high moorland guard the western flank of the Black Mountains. The two outliers of Mynydd Troed and Mynydd Llangorse are not the highest peaks in the range. But their shapely profiles garner broad open tops, carpeted in heather and bracken, with firm grassy tracks and views extending in all directions. Here are 8 miles of real freedom and some of the best walking in the Black Mountains. The two mountains are deeply cleft by Cwm Sorgwm, host to a diminutive tributary of the Rhiangoll. Walk 19 (3¾ miles) and Walk 20 (4¼ miles) can be tackled separately or as a figure of eight, with the 'crossover' at the head Cwm Sorgwm. Here a narrow road reaches the pass between Mynydd Troed and Mynydd Llangorse.

WALK 19
MYNYDD TROED

START Castle Inn, Pengenffordd SO 174297.
DIRECTIONS The Castle Inn is situated just south of the highest point on the A479 between Abergavenny and Talgarth. There is a large pub car park on the southbound side of the road, immediately north of the Castle Inn. Non-patrons are asked to pay a small charge for parking at the pub, which is given to charity.

1 From the northern end of the car park at the Castle Inn, follow the footpath sign to Castell Dinas, leading down some steps to a bridleway. TURN LEFT and follow the track as it runs parallel to the main road as a safer alternative. After about 400 yards, come to a junction with a small lane. TURN LEFT here, crossing the main road and taking the track opposite around the back of some farm buildings. At the back of the barns, BEAR LEFT through a gate on to an old tree-lined track. After a short distance another gate leads on to the open hillside. BEAR LEFT crossing an area of old pits and pick up a narrow but distinct path that tackles the north ridge of Mynydd Troed head on. Although not as high as its loftier neighbours to the east, this is still a steep, unremitting ascent and you climb over 700 feet in half a mile. The middle section is the steepest on this walk, and in the entire book! But, mist permitting, you can pause to enjoy views of the central massif of the Black Mountains and you can clearly see the old ramparts of Castell Dinas rising above the Castle Inn *(see Walk 5)*.

2 A trig point (609 metres) marks the summit and the highest point of the walk. The characteristic outline of Llangorse Lake (Llyn Syfaddan) lies below. *Llangorse Lake is the largest natural stretch of water in southern Wales. Popular with both boats and birds, it is protected as a wildlife sanctuary. It also has a long historical pedigree, with the remains of an ancient lake settlement.* Continue on a narrow path along the edge of the steep escarpment, in a south westerly direction. It soon descends steeply as it aims for the head of Cwm Sorgwm. Beyond this valley you can see the route ahead as it climbs the next ridge to Mynydd Llangorse. A short way down, an alternative path from the summit crosses the way. But maintain your direction, taking care as the path is grassy and very steep. The gradient eases as you approach the narrow road at Blaen-sorgwm. TURN RIGHT in front of the gate (unless you would like to continue up Mynydd Llangorse on Walk 20 from point 3).

3 Follow the grassy path around the western side of Mynydd Troed, at first by the fence. Maintain this contour and avoid the temptation to descend when the fence veers left on a couple of occasions. The route circumnavigates the base of Mynydd Troed and brings you back to the mountain gate at the beginning of your initial ascent. Follow your outward route back to the Castle Inn.

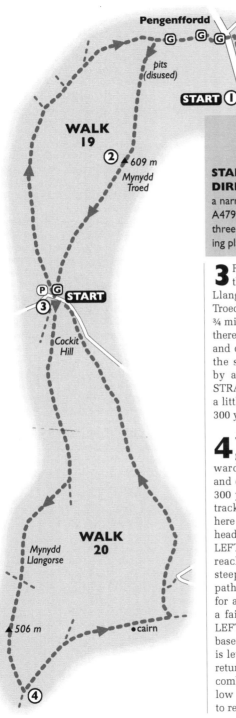

WALK 20
MYNYDD LLANGORSE

START Blaen-sorgwm SO 161283.
DIRECTIONS Blaen-sorgwm is at the top of a narrow minor road between Llangorse and the A479 near Cwmdu. There is space for two or three cars but be careful not to block the passing place.

3 From the road climb the broad grassy path that mounts the south ridge of Mynydd Llangorse. This is not as steep as Mynydd Troed, but it's still a steady pull. After about ¾ mile and after you have gained the plateau, there is a junction in the path. BEAR RIGHT and continue on the gently climbing track to the summit of Mynydd Llangorse, marked by a trig point at 506 metres. Continue STRAIGHT AHEAD on the track which loses a little height to reach a broad junction about 300 yards after the summit.

4 TURN SHARP LEFT here and follow the grassy track through the bracken northwards. Enjoy the exhilarating wide views and open freedom of the ridge. After another 300 yards or so, come to another junction of tracks marked by a signpost. BEAR RIGHT here to take the track that curves around the head of Cwm Sorgwm. In about ¼ mile BEAR LEFT in front of a large cairn. The path soon reaches the edge of the plateau and drops steeply down the side. Half way down the path TURN SHARP LEFT. (Ignore the sign for a bridle way that leads straight on along a fainter path here). At the bottom, TURN LEFT to follow the track running along the base of the hillside, just above the fields. This is level at first and then ascends gradually to return to the road at Blaen-sorgwm. If you've combined this walk with Mynydd Troed, follow the instructions from point 3 on Walk 19 to return to Pengenffordd.

Just in case...

If you are undertaking a high-level walk, regardless of the time of year, you need to be properly equipped. Welsh weather is often fickle, and what begins as a fine day can finish with rain, or snow, or mist, or wind. So take a comfortable and waterproof rucksack (or line it with a plastic sack) and *ensure you use, or have with you,* the following basic gear at all times:

- waterproof jacket with a hood, and water proof trousers
- walking boots (with gaiters if you wish)
- warm and comfortable socks, and a hat
- light but warm sweater and trousers
- windproof gloves or mittens
- high energy food, and water

- a map, pencil and compass
- basic first aid kit
- Swiss Army Knife or multi-tool
- *and you can add any comfort items, plus a camera, mobile phone (fully charged!), sunglasses and so on as you wish (but keep your rucksack as light as possible)*

KEY TO THE MAPS

——— Main road

——— Minor road

•━▶━ Walk route & direction

① Walk instruction

— — — Adjoining path

∿ River or stream

Ⓖ Gate

Ⓢ Stile

▲ Summit

🌲🌳 Woods or forest

🍺 Pub

Ⓟ Parking

THE COUNTRYSIDE CODE

- Be safe – plan ahead and follow any signs

- Leave gates and property as you find them

- Protect plants and animals, and take your litter home

- Keep dogs under close control

- Consider other people

The CroW Act 2000, implemented throughout Wales in May 2005, introduced new legal rights of access for walkers to designated open country, predominantly mountain, moor, heath or down, plus all registered common land. This access can be subject to restrictions and closure for land management or safety reasons for up to 28 days a year.

Published by
Kittiwake
3 Glantwymyn Village Workshops, Glantwymyn, Machynlleth, Montgomeryshire SY20 8LY

© Text: Alastair Ross 2011
© Maps & illustrations: Kittiwake 2011
Drawings by Morag Perrott
Cover photographs – *Main:* Near Talgarth.
Inset: Llanthony Priory. Alastair Ross.

Printed by MWL, Pontypool.
First edition 2006. Revised edition 2007. Reprinted twice 2007. Minor revisions 2008. Reprinted twice 2009. New edition 2011.
ISBN: **978 1 902302 92 8**